rebel lives **louise michel** rebel lives **louise michel** rebel lives

also published in the **rebel lives** series:

Helen Keller, *edited by John Davis*
Haydée Santamaría, *edited by Betsy Maclean*
Albert Einstein, *edited by Jim Green*
Sacco & Vanzetti, *edited by John Davis*

forthcoming in the **rebel lives** series:

Ho Chi Minh, *edited by Alexandra Keeble*
Chris Hani, *edited by Thenjiwe Mtintso*

rebel lives, a fresh new series of inexpensive, accessible and provoca-
tive books unearthing the rebel histories of some familiar figures and
introducing some lesser-known rebels

rebel lives, selections of writings by and about remarkable women
and men whose radicalism has been concealed or forgotten. Edited and
introduced by activists and researchers around the world, the series
presents stirring accounts of race, class and gender rebellion

rebel lives does not seek to canonize its subjects as perfect political
models, visionaries or martyrs, but to make available the ideas and
stories of imperfect revolutionary human beings to a new generation of
readers and aspiring rebels

louise michel

edited by Nic Maclellan

Ocean Press
Melbourne ■ New York
www.oceanbooks.com.au

rebel lives

Cover design by Sean Walsh and Meaghan Barbuto

ISBN: 1-876175-76-1
Library of Congress Control No: 2004100834
First Printed in 2004

Published by Ocean Press

Australia: GPO Box 3279, Melbourne, Victoria 3001, Australia
Fax: (61-3) 9329 5040 Tel: (61-3) 9326 4280
E-mail: info@oceanbooks.com.au

USA: PO Box 1186, Old Chelsea Station, New York, NY 10113-1186, USA

Ocean Press Distributors:

United States and Canada: **Consortium Book Sales and Distribution**
Tel: 1-800-283-3572   www.cbsd.com

Britain and Europe: **Pluto Books**
E-mail: pluto@plutobooks.com

Australia and New Zealand: **Palgrave Macmillan**
E-mail: customer.service@macmillan.com.au

Cuba and Latin America: **Ocean Press**
E-mail: oceanhav@enet.cu

www.oceanbooks.com.au

contents

chapter six: *"The Internationale"*

chapter seven: *Exile in New Caledonia*

chapter eight: *Authority Vested in One Person is a Crime*

chapter nine: *Emma and Louise*

resources

introduction

In France, Louise Michel is celebrated as the heroine of the Paris Commune of 1871. Schools, railway stations and streets are named after her. In recent years, a number of new biographies have documented her legendary life, and over a thousand of her letters have been collated and published.

But outside France her history and legacy are not widely known. Louise Michel receives fleeting references in most histories of the Commune, when the people of Paris rose up between March and May 1871 to establish a short-lived workers' government in the city. But after the Commune was crushed, Michel was captured, imprisoned and exiled to the other side of the world. From there, she disappears from most histories of the 19th century.

Beyond the tumultuous days of the Paris Commune, however, Louise Michel continued to lead a life of rebellion and hope.

Inspired by a mixture of anarchist, anticlerical and republican values, Michel maintained her rebel spirit for the last 30 years of her life, until her death in Marseilles in January 1905, aged 74. She spoke, campaigned and demonstrated in support of social revolution and women's rights in France and neighboring European countries.

Throughout her later life, Michel was an internationalist. She supported anticolonial struggles in the French colonies of Africa, Indochina and the Pacific islands. In her South Pacific exile, she stood against the racism of her fellow deportees, supporting the 1878 revolt by the indigenous Kanak population of New Caledonia against French colonization. In the last decades of the 19th century, she campaigned for the rights of Algerians who rose against French rule, paving the way for later generations of French pacifists and socialists who supported Algeria's National Liberation Front in 1954–62.

She was a teacher, a writer, a poet and a defiant orator who inspired others to write poems and eulogies in her honor. And during her life, Louise Michel maintained a lively correspondence with poets and writers, scientists and anarchists, drunkards and loved ones.

Early life

Louise Michel was born on May 29, 1830, in the small village of Vroncourt in the Haute-Marne region of France. Her mother, Marie-Anne Michel, worked as a servant for the landowner Étienne-Charles Demahis. Marie-Anne was unmarried, and many writers suggest that Louise's father was Demahis' son Laurent — throughout her life, in fact, Michel regarded the older Demahis as her own grandparents.

From an early age, Michel was encouraged to read and question by these grandparents. She wanted to be a writer, and throughout her life composed a variety of poems, essays, theater scripts and stories — often unreadable, always passionate. She began writing to the famous author Victor Hugo, known throughout the world for his books *Les Misérables* and *The Hunchback of Notre Dame,* and they formed a lifetime friendship.

Her critique of society drew on Catholic values, her love of animals and observations of rural life (see Chapter Two). As her *Memoirs* explain:

> As far back as I can remember, the origin of my revolt against the powerful was my horror at the tortures inflicted on animals. I used to wish animals could get revenge, that the dog could bite the man who was mercilessly beating him, that the horse bleeding under the whip could throw off the man tormenting him.

Michel left home after the death of her grandparents and arguments with Laurent Demahis' wife, who denounced her as a "bastard." At age 21, she began studying to be a primary schoolteacher and in September 1852, she became head teacher at a school in Audeloncourt in Haute-Marne. (She later claimed that she opened her own school to avoid pledging allegiance to Emperor Napoleon III, as was required for public schoolteachers.) She traveled to Paris the next year to teach, but returned to Haute-Marne after several months when her mother fell sick.

Over the next few years, Michel taught at small schools at Clefmont and Millières in the Haute-Marne region. She experimented in libertarian teaching methods, using techniques ahead of her time: composing plays for her students to perform and bringing animals and birds into class for the children to touch. As one colleague noted:

> I can't say it was entirely proper, as the Sorbonne understands the word. It was something of a free-for-all, with highly unusual teaching methods, but taking everything into account, you had to agree that instruction was being offered.

Yet she continued to dream of Paris. It was only in 1865 that she had enough funds to open a day school in the capital, after selling some land left to her by the Demahis family.

Struggle against the empire

As a provincial schoolteacher, Louise Michel was not actively engaged in the turbulent politics of the mid-19th century. Throughout Europe, the year 1848 was marked by popular and republican uprisings — in France, a republic was declared. But in 1851, the short-lived French Republic was overthrown in a coup d'état by Charles Louis Napoleon Bonaparte (nephew of the famous general).

Louis Napoleon's Second Empire lasted until 1870, with support from the conservative rural peasantry. By the end of his reign, however, popular opposition to the empire was rising. During the 1860s, many elections in urban centers were won by republicans — both middle-class reformers and working-class radicals. On January 12, 1870, nearly 100,000 people demonstrated against the Second Empire after a republican journalist Victor Noir was killed by Prince Pierre Bonaparte, the emperor's cousin. Louise Michel attended the funeral dressed as a man, carrying a dagger beneath her clothes.

In July 1870, after a diplomatic struggle over a Prussian attempt to take control of the vacant Spanish throne, the French Emperor declared war on Prussia. In August, three Prussian armies invaded France. Using new technologies (railways and rapid-firing artillery), they soon defeated French Marshal MacMahon at Worth and Weissenburg and surrounded the city of Strasbourg. In mid-August, French forces were defeated at Mars-la-Tour and Gravelotte, and the Prussians advanced on Chalons.

After the decisive Prussian victory at the battle of Sedan, Emperor Louis Napoleon III and Marshal MacMahon were captured, capitulating on September 2 with over 83,000 soldiers. At news of the Sedan defeat, workers in Paris invaded the Bourbon Palace and forced the Legislative Assembly to proclaim the fall of the empire and declare a republic on September 4. A provisional Government of National Defense was established to continue the war to remove the Prussians from France: "not an inch of our soil, not a stone of our fortresses, will we cede."

Just a few years earlier in 1864, the German revolutionary Karl Marx helped found the International Working Men's Association in London (a network later called the First International). Now, a series of meetings and demonstrations began in London and other European cities, calling for recognition of the new French Republic. The General Council of the First International took a direct part in this solidarity movement, organizing resolutions and petitions calling on the British Government to immediately recognize the republic.

Early political activism

During this upheaval, Louise Michel was drawn into the political activity that would consume the rest of her life.

In Paris, Michel had begun to read texts on natural history, chemistry and scientific philosophy, including Charles Darwin's *Origin of the Species*, and declared herself to be an atheist and a materialist. She joined the Union of Poets and maintained an extensive correspondence with cultural figures such as writer Victor Hugo, poet Paul Verlaine and other French artists. She also met a range of republican and revolutionary leaders who would play a key role in the Paris Commune, such as Théophile Ferré (the socialist agitator whom she most admired — even loved — but who was executed in November 1871 after the fall of the Commune).

On August 15, 1870, Louise Michel joined a demonstration in support of Generals Emile Eudes and Brideau, two republicans arrested by the government. She carried a petition in their favor to General Trochu, the military governor of Paris. In September, Louise Michel hit public notice with her calls for "free thinking citizens" to provide nursing and medical support to the town of Strasbourg, which had been encircled by the Prussian Army for over a month:

> The idea came to some among us — or rather, some women among us, for we women were in the majority — to get weapons and set forth to help Strasbourg defend itself, and to die with it.

She was a member of two vigilance committees established in the 18th arrondissement in the eastern suburbs of Paris — one for men and the other for women. In November, she was elected president of the Women's Vigilance Committee:

> I spent the finest hours of the siege with the Montmartre Vigilance Committee and with the Club de la Patrie en Danger. One was a little more fully alive there, with the feeling of being in one's element, in the midst of the intense struggle for liberty.

The Prussian military advance continued in late 1870. Paris was besieged from September 19, and the Government of National Defense moved to the city of Versailles. The French Army of over 150,000 men surrendered on October 27, but when the Government of National Defense started negotiations with the Prussians, Paris workers and sections of the National Guard rose up in revolt, led by the socialist revolutionary Louis Auguste Blanqui. They seized the Paris Town Hall and set up a revolutionary government — the Committee of Public Safety — which lasted for just days before Blanqui was arrested and charged with treason.

Between October 1870 and March 1871, the Government of National Defense and the radical republican forces in Paris vied for political supremacy. The republican National Guard was established as a popular militia, effectively arming the workers of Paris. The National Guard enlisted 384,000 men in 234 neighborhood battalions and also established a women's battalion led by Colonel Adelaide Valentin.

Louise Michel was swept up in this revolutionary ferment. She participated in the massive demonstration on October 31, 1870, in front of the Paris Town Hall to support the Committee of Public Safety. In December, she was arrested for the first time, following a women's demonstration at the Paris Town Hall that called for the training and recruitment of women for the National Guard. And on January 22, 1871, dressed in a National Guard uniform and armed with a rifle, Louise Michel returned fire on troops under the command of Versailles General Trochu when they shot at a crowd protesting in front of the Town Hall.

Louise Michel even argued with other radicals, suggesting that she should travel to Versailles to assassinate Adolphe Thiers, the reactionary leader of the Government of National Defense. Although persuaded that an act of terror would only bring reprisals, she traveled to Versailles in disguise and returned to Paris to prove it could be done.

The Government of National Defense moved to surrender to the encircling Prussian forces, agreeing to pay five billion francs and hand over much of the border provinces of Alsace and Lorraine. But the surrender would only take effect if Paris could be controlled.

Before dawn on March 18, 1871, the Versailles Government sent 4,000 troops to seize the cannons held by the National Guard. Many of these guns were stationed on the Butte of Montmartre — the bluffs overlooking the city — and the suburb where Louise Michel was an active member of the Women's Committee. As she describes in her *Memoirs* (see Chapter Three), Michel helped rally women to seize the National Guard cannon and stop the Versailles troops from dragging them away. The troops refused to fire on the women, and instead arrested and shot their own commander!

Delegates of the National Guard found themselves in effective political control of the city, and elections were called within a week. The Paris Commune had begun its revolt.

Popular control in the Commune

So what was the Commune? In French, the term means local municipality, but for the men and women of 1871, it also recalled the Commune created during the French Revolution in 1792 — a symbol of popular control.

On March 26, 1871, a week after the attempted seizure of the National Guard's cannon, over 229,000 citizens of Paris elected an 80-member municipal council. The Paris Commune consisted of middle-class republicans as well as more radical workers and shopkeepers. Nearly half the elected members of the Commune were skilled workers, while others were journalists, lawyers, doctors and accountants. Most were supporters of the republican left — almost 20 percent were members of Marx's First International, while others were followers of the anarchist leader Pierre-Joseph Proudhon (including the fabric designer Eugène Pottier, who was later to write the revolutionary hymn "The Internationale"). Louise Michel's suburb Montmartre was a hotbed of working-class and revolutionary ferment, with 15,000 of 17,000 eligible voters supporting the jailed socialist Auguste Blanqui.

In its short life between March and May 1871, the Commune enacted a series of decrees to promote radical democracy — policies on security, democracy and economy that led to its celebration as the first workers' government. These included:

Security: The Paris uprising marked a revolt against the old symbols of militarism and repression. The first decision of the Commune was to abolish conscription and the standing army, leaving the National Guard militia as the sole armed force. The guillotine was publicly burnt by National Guard troops, amid great popular rejoicing. On May 16, in the dying days of the Commune, the Victory Column on the Place Vendôme (cast from guns captured by Napoleon after the war of 1809) was demolished as a "symbol of chauvinism and incitement to national hatred."

Democracy: The Commune decreed the separation of church from state, the abolition of all state payments for religious purposes and the transfer of all church property into national property. The decree ordered the removal of all religious symbols, pictures, dogmas and prayers from schools — "all that belongs to the sphere of the individual's conscience."

Key administrative, judicial and educational positions were filled by popular election rather than appointment, and members of the Commune were forbidden to hold multiple positions. Foreigners elected to the Commune were confirmed in office, because "the flag of the Commune is the flag of the World Republic."

Economy: Other reforms opened the way for working people to seize economic power. In light of the economic collapse brought on by the war and siege of Paris, the Commune moved to shift the tax burden away from workers, tradespeople, artisans and small businesses, decreeing a moratorium on debt foreclosures, postponing debt obligations for three years and supporting the abolition of interest on debts. Pension rights were extended to common-law wives and children, a challenge to church values and propriety.

In one of its few explicitly socialist steps, on April 16, the Commune issued a decree on abandoned factories, so that people could form cooperatives and work in factories deserted by their owners who had fled the revolution.

The Commune also decided that its elected members could only receive a salary of up to 6,000 francs — similar to that of other workers. A decree abolished night work for bakers, ended the unpopular system of workers' registration cards and ordered the closing of pawnshops as "a private exploitation of labor."

Women in the Commune

Throughout the Commune, Parisians organized themselves into local community clubs, and these popular associations became centers of debate, theater and publishing. After the creation of the Commune in March 1871, Louise Michel regularly participated in meetings of the (men's) Vigilance Committee in Montmartre and immersed herself in support work for children, women's groups and community associations.

As chair of the Women's Vigilance Committee, she played a leading role in mobilizing women in support of the Commune, and organized day care for 200 children living in besieged Paris. She recruited women as ambulance workers, even among the sex workers from her suburb. Rejecting her male compatriots' concern that "the wounded must be tended by pure hands," she argued:

> Who has more right than these women, the most pitiful of the old order's victims, to give their life for the new?

Women's activists like Sophie Poirier and the 20-year-old Russian revolutionary Elisabeth Dmitrieff moved beyond more basic demands, putting forward socialist proposals to the leaders of the Paris Commune. Poirier established a workshop employing over 70 women, all of whom shared in the profits.

These radicals called for the seizure of deserted factories for use by the women who worked in them (see Chapter Four). Their demands — equal pay for equal work, better occupational health and safety, a reduction in working hours — still resonate today. In response, some Commune decrees directly addressed women's status, such as a decree on May 21 that granted equal pay to male and female teachers.

The example of the Paris Commune

The Paris Commune, which only lasted between March 18 and May 28, 1871, has assumed legendary importance. It inspired a range of anarchists, socialists and communists in the decades leading up to the Russian Revolution of 1917, and was a source of ideas about the replacement of capitalist political structures with those that could assist a transition to a socialist society.

The Paris uprising is celebrated as the first great workers' revolt to challenge the power of the state and form a workers' government. This legacy comes even though many of its decrees and actions were not fully implemented, given the short period of popular control of the city, and many of the Commune leaders were not workers, socialists or revolutionaries.

From his exile in London, Karl Marx closely followed events in Paris. Just days after the uprising, he published *The Civil War in France,* a report for the General Council of the First International. This famous text analyzed the importance of the short-lived Commune and challenged the notion that ordinary workers are not equipped to govern. The pamphlet was a scathing polemical attack on Adolphe Thiers — the "monstrous gnome," "a parliamentary Tom Thumb," "a monkey allowed for a time to give full vent to his tigerish instinct." Before the end of the year, it had been published in 30 editions in 11 languages.

Marx suggested that the Commune represented a significant new breakthrough in creating a workers' government, rather than one led by middle-class republicans:

> This was the first revolution in which the working class was openly acknowledged as the only class capable of social initiative, even by the great bulk of the Paris middle class — shopkeepers, tradesmen, merchants — the wealthy capitalists alone excepted.

In an April 1871 letter sent to a colleague in the First International, Marx argued: "History has no like example of greatness. With the struggle in Paris, the struggle of the working class against the capitalist class and its state has entered a new phase."

Marx and his collaborator Friedrich Engels argued that the Commune raised crucial issues for any radical movement. In 1872, in a new introduction to their revolutionary *Communist Manifesto*, they argued that a workers' revolution would have to "smash the state machine" before it could progress any further: "One thing especially was proved by the Commune… that the working class cannot simply lay hold of the ready-made state machinery and wield it for its own purposes."

Repression of the Communards

This republican, anticlerical and popular rebellion struck fear in both the Prussian Army and the reactionary French Government of National Defense. Versailles leader Adolphe Thiers asked Prussian Chancellor Otto von Bismarck for permission to build up the Versailles Army with French prisoners of war who had surrendered after the Prussian victories at Sedan and Metz. Bismarck agreed after the payment of a massive indemnity, and the French Army began a siege of Paris.

From April 3, 1871, the Versailles troops launched a final assault to crush the Paris Commune. As a member of the 61st Montmartre battalion, Louise Michel participated in the defense of Paris, both as a fighter and a medical worker.

The image of Louise Michel as warrior is often highlighted in histories of the Commune, ignoring her achievements as poet and politician. But there is no doubt that she was on the barricades in the defense of Paris. She fought in battles at Clamart, Neuilly and Issy-les-Moulineaux, and her courage is mentioned specifically in the Commune's official *Journal* on April 10: "An energetic woman has been fighting in the ranks of the 61st Battalion, and has killed several police and soldiers."

In between the fighting, she read the works of Baudelaire and played the harmonium at a church near Neuilly. But in her own *Memoirs*, she writes:

> Yes, barbarian that I was, I loved the cannon, the smell of gunpowder and grapeshot in the air, but above all, I was in love with the revolution!

Versailles troops entered Paris on May 21, after Prussian troops who held the northern and eastern forts allowed the French troops to cross land to the north of the city. In the wealthier suburbs, the Versailles troops were welcomed as liberators, but resistance was fiercer as they approached the working-class suburbs. As Paris burned, Communard women were denounced as *petroleuses* (incendiaries or arsonists), a charge later hurled at Louise Michel by the conservative press.

In the final days of conflict, the Communards executed a number of military, church and political hostages, for which they were pilloried by the Versailles press. But these deaths were overshadowed by the ferocity of the Versailles troops, who spent eight days massacring workers and shooting many civilians on sight. An English eyewitness noted the resistance of Michel's women's battalion:

> They fought like devils, far better than the men; and I had the pain of seeing 52 shot down, even when they had been surrounded by the troops and disarmed.

Thousands of Communards and workers were summarily executed. The exact number of dead is unknown, but more than 20,000 were killed, with 43,000 others arrested, tens of thousands imprisoned and nearly 5,000 later deported. A March 1872 law banned the First International as subversive, and all socialist and anarchist activity was illegal for over a decade.

Today, at the Père Lachaise cemetery in Paris, a small plaque marks the wall where the final Communards who surrendered were gunned down — "Aux Morts de la Commune, 21–28 mai, 1871" (To the dead of the Commune). The cemetery is best known to tourists as the resting place for the singer of The Doors, Jim Morrison, but the corner near the Commune plaque is surrounded by the graves of French revolutionaries, including anti-Nazi Resistance fighters, trade unionists and socialist and communist activists.

Trial and deportation

Louise Michel escaped the final massacre of the Communards. On May 18, she had been sent to work with the Vigilance Committee in Montmartre. She fought at the Montmartre cemetery and on the barricades at Clignancourt, where she took part in the last resistance against the advancing Versailles troops. At first she evaded capture, but when her mother was taken hostage she turned herself in. Soon after, she was transferred to Versailles and brought before a military tribunal for interrogation.

In September 1871, Michel was transferred to the Arras prison, where she was held for over two months until her trial. On December 16, 1871, Louise Michel appeared before the 4th Council of War. As detailed in Chapter Eight, Michel had little respect for any court of law. She scorned the authority of the military tribunal, stating:

Louise Michel: Since it seems that any heart which beats for liberty has the right only to a small lump of lead, I demand my share. If you let me live, I will not stop crying for vengeance, and I will denounce the assassins on the Board of Pardons to avenge my brothers.

President of the Court: I cannot allow you to continue speaking if you continue in this tone.

Louise Michel: I have finished… If you are not cowards, kill me.

Her defiance made the front page of newspapers around France, and Victor Hugo wrote the poem "Viro Major" in her honor. But the judges rejected her offer of martyrdom. Instead, the court condemned her to deportation within a fortress in New Caledonia, the French South Pacific colony 20,000 miles from Paris. She refused to appeal the decision, and was detained in France for nearly two years awaiting deportation.

On August 24, 1873, she joined other Communards who were transferred by train through Paris to the port of La Rochelle. Four days later, 169 deportees — 20 of them women — were loaded onto the vessel *Virginie* for the four-month voyage to the South Pacific.

Among the Kanaks

Just 1,800 kilometers off the east coast of Australia, the islands of New Caledonia became Louise Michel's exile for more than six years.

After the annexation of New Caledonia in 1853, France established a penal colony that remained the cornerstone of colonial society until its closure in 1897. As well as criminals, the convoys brought Algerian prisoners after the defeat of the 1871 uprising led by Abd-el Kader, together with political prisoners after the crushing of the Paris Commune. Over 4,200 Communards were deported to New Caledonia, with 20 convoys traveling between September 29, 1872, and October 25, 1878.

Louise Michel arrived in New Caledonia on December 10, 1873. The leaders of the Commune, like Henri Rochfort, were initially detained on the Ducos peninsula at Numbo. Together with other women of the Commune, Michel refused to be separated from her male comrades, and was also detained in the camp at Ducos (see letter, Chapter Seven).

She had extensive political discussions with anarchists such as Nathalie Lemel and Charles Malato, and it was during her exile that Michel adopted the anarchist politics that she would follow for the rest of her life. Her friendship with Rochford was also to last throughout her life, and he continued to support Michel financially even as their politics diverged in later years.

The colonial administration in New Caledonia granted immigrants the best land in the plains and the low valleys. As their land was taken, the indigenous Melanesian population known as Kanaks was pushed back into the narrow valleys of the interior, where it was difficult to grow staple foods like yam and taro.

Louise Michel took up defense of the Kanak cause: "To some comrades I seemed to be more Kanak than the Kanaks" (see Chapter Seven). From an early fascination with cannibalism, she started to learn some of the indigenous Kanak languages, and worked as a teacher with Kanak children and adults. Michel's style of teaching soon raised the ire of one prison administrator, who stated:

> You must close your school. You're filling the heads of these Canaques with pernicious doctrines. The other day, you were heard talking about humanity, justice, freedom and other useless things.

Gradually, she collected Kanak legends, chants and songs, which were published in the local newspaper *Les Petits Affiches*, and collated and republished on her return to Paris.

From the 1840s, Kanak clans had sporadically resisted the theft of their land. The policy of *cantonment,* imposed systematically from 1876 onwards, contributed to the great uprising of 1878 led by Chief Atai. Atai was famous for his declaration against the theft of Kanak land: "When my taro can go and eat on the land where your cows graze, I will respect your enclosures."

With many clans following Atai, this rebellion continued for two months in the west of the main island, around colonial centers like La Foa, Bourail and Bouloupari. Isolated farms were attacked, and some 200 colonists were killed. Repression by the French Army was fierce, and continued for over six months, causing more than 1,200 deaths among the Kanaks, of whom Atai was one — betrayed by opposing clans.

During the 1878 revolt, most of the Communards exiled in New Caledonia rallied to the French state. But Louise Michel sided with the Kanaks, identifying with their spirit of rebellion:

> The Kanaks were seeking the same liberty we had sought in the Commune. Let me say only that my red scarf, the red scarf of the Commune that I had hidden from every search, was divided in two pieces one night. Two Kanaks, before going to join the insurgents against the whites, had come to say goodbye to me. [Then] they slipped into the ocean. The sea was bad, and they may never have arrived across the bay, or perhaps they were killed in the fighting. I never saw either of them again, and I don't know which of the two deaths took them, but they were brave with the bravery that black and white both have.

The symbolism of Louise Michel's gesture lives on in the modern Kanak movement for independence. In the early 1970s, a new generation of Kanak students returned home after studying in France during the turmoil of May 1968. To campaign for independence from France, they formed a group called the Foulards Rouges — the Red Scarves. Today, Michel's writings on Kanak culture are republished in New Caledonia, a primary school has been named after her and "The Red Virgin," a play in her honor, was performed at the Tjibaou Cultural Center in 2002.

Solidarity with Algeria

Louise Michel's internationalism was also expressed in her solidarity with the 1871 Kabyle uprising in Algeria, where 200,000 people rose up against French rule — a revolt crushed by 80,000 French troops. Michel's *Memoirs* noted:

> In the first days after our deportation, one morning we saw the arrival — in their great white burnous — of the Arabs deported, like us, for having risen up against oppression. These Orientals,

who have been jailed far from their tents and their flocks, are so simple and good and of great merit.

Michel's solidarity with the Kanaks and Algerians stood out against the prevailing racism of the settler community in Noumea and even among many exiled Communards, and in her *Memoirs*, Michel recalls friends made among the Algerian deportees.

In December 1879, Louise Michel was offered a reduction in her sentence, which she initially refused. However, in July 1880, an amnesty decree was issued in France for members of the Commune and Michel was pardoned. Arriving in Australia on her way home, she requested passage to France on a fast mail carrier rather than a slow sailing ship to get to her mother's side more quickly. Her request was initially refused, but in her *Memoirs* she describes how she encouraged the French Consul to speed her passage:

> The French Consul at Sydney had not yet made up his mind to repatriate me with some others scheduled to go on the mail ship. I told him that, in that case, I would be obliged to give lectures on the Commune for several days, so that I could use the fees for my trip. He then decided to send me with 20 others on the mail ship *John Helder* which was leaving for London.

She arrived in London on November 7, 1880, then two days later made a triumphal return to the Saint-Lazare station in Paris.

Radical agitation

For the remainder of her life, Louise Michel continued to agitate for radical and anarchist causes. Her profile as a former Communard ensured wide public attention and popular affection, and she often spoke with tempestuous fury: "The ocean of revolutions will carry us forward with its high tides."

The British historian of anarchism, George Woodcock, described her as a "secular saint." But for conservatives, Louise Michel became the symbol of all things ugly and threatening. In caricatures and polemics, right-wing newspapers dubbed her "the Red Virgin," presenting her as unattractive and masculine.

Ironically, her supporters have taken up this title with pride, and new generations of feminist writers have speculated on her sexuality and her refusal to marry. In many recent studies of Michel's life, writers ponder her admiration for Victor Hugo (old enough to be her father), her unfulfilled love for the executed Communard Théophile Ferré, and her close relations with women such as Miriam Ferré and Nathalie Lemel. Scholars scour her letters for evidence to back up theories that her return to Haute-Marne from Paris was to bear Hugo's child, or that her break with Lemel may have come after the end of a lesbian relationship.

Clearly, information about Michel's private life is scarce. There is, however, plenty of evidence that Louise Michel was a passionate orator and agitator. Throughout the 1880s and 1890s, Louise Michel spoke at numerous public meetings in support of radical causes, workers' struggles and for the rights of the unemployed. She was often called on to present tributes to her comrades from the Paris Commune — soon after her return to Paris, in January 1881, she delivered the eulogy at the funeral of socialist leader Blanqui.

She was willing to speak from the stage with a range of radicals, but her commitment was to "social revolution," deeply opposed to parliamentary politics. Although she was a strong supporter of women taking their place in society, she did not support the 19th century feminist demand for the vote for women — she also opposed the vote for men! Her emotional ties were with the anarchist movement. The *Manifesto of the Anarchists*, published in January 1883, states: "Villains that we are, we claim bread for all, knowledge for all, work for all, independence and justice for all!"

For Louise Michel: "I share all the ideas written there."

On her return from New Caledonia, she published a number of volumes about Kanak culture and the history of the Commune, and the publication of her *Memoirs* in 1886 gave a wider audience to her views. She wrote for many workers' and socialist newsletters and, together with anarchist Sebastian Faure, founded the journal *Le Libertaire* in November 1895.

She maintained her internationalist perspective, and condemned French military operations in its overseas colonies: "In 1871, the government's abattoirs were in Paris, now they're in Madagascar and Tonkin." In 1880, hundreds of former Communards met at a hall in Varigaud, calling for amnesty for the 1871 Algerian rebels who had risen up against the French — Louise Michel was chosen as one of two honorary chairs for the conference. She supported this amnesty campaign for 15 years until the final granting of pardons in 1895. In 1904, just before her death, she traveled to Algeria to investigate the situation of Arabs in the French colony.

Police harassment

Her adulation by many working-class supporters was matched by close attention from the police. In the 25 years after her return from exile, the authorities of several European countries monitored her speeches and regularly arrested, jailed or deported her. In one letter to a friend, she added a postscript:

> Would the people responsible for opening my mail please reseal the letters and put them in the post! As you've seen, we're not talking about you.

Chapter Eight details her constant run-ins with the law, such as a two-week stint in prison in January 1882 for insulting police.

On March 9, 1883, Louise Michel took part in a rally of unemployed people at Les Invalides in Paris, during which some bakeries were looted. As Michel and fellow anarchist Emile Pouget had been carrying a black flag at the front of the rally, police issued a warrant for her arrest. She dodged the police for two weeks (see letter in Chapter Eight) but on March 29, she wrote to Police Commissioner Camescasse, saying she would hand herself in, and the next day she was arrested and taken to Saint-Lazare prison. In this prison, she met a number of prostitutes, and later took up the cause of sex workers, seeing them as the victims of sexual exploitation: "No more girls for prostitution, no more boys for the army…"

At her trial for the Les Invalides protest on June 21, the prosecutor asked: "Do you take part in every demonstration that occurs?"

Her reply: "Unfortunately, yes. I am always on the side of the wretched!"

After a fiery speech to the judges (see Chapter Eight), she was sentenced to six years' solitary detention, followed by 10 years monitoring by the police, and transferred to the Clermont-de-l'Oise prison. The severity of the sentence shocked many, including the poet Paul Verlaine, who wrote his "Ballad in Honor of Louise Michel."

Her prison sentence was cut short after the death of her mother on January 3, 1885. Three days after her mother's funeral, a presidential decree offered Michel a pardon. At first she refused, then later accepted, and was free again to continue her agitation.

Her public speaking continued to provoke the authorities. On June 3, 1886, Michel spoke with socialist leaders Jules Guesde, Paul Lafargue and Dr. Susini at a public meeting in Paris, in favor of striking miners from Decazeville. In August, together with her radical colleagues, she was sentenced to four months in prison and a 100 franc fine for speaking in favor of the miners. The next month, Guesde, Lafargue and Susini successfully appealed the court's decision and were released. But Louise refused to appeal, embarrassing the government with her defiance. After various contortions by the government, she was pardoned in November 1886.

Her closest call came in January 1888, after a speech at the Gaîté theater in Le Havre. That evening, a Catholic fanatic Pierre Lucas fired his pistol twice and wounded Michel in the head. Nevertheless, she protected Lucas from the angry crowd and later refused to lodge a complaint against him — a symbol of her contempt for the police and justice system.

Trouble came again following a May Day speech Michel gave in the French town of Vienne on April 30, 1890. Michel was arrested after protesting workers, carrying red and black flags, clashed with police, set up barricades in the town and looted a factory. She refused to accept an offer of provisional release unless all her co-accused were released. Although her arrest warrant was revoked, she smashed up her cell and refused to leave the prison unless her conditions were met. The hospital doctors declared her insane (a common tactic used against rebel women), but fearing a scandal the government released her, returning her to Paris on June 4.

Fearful that the authorities would use the insanity declaration to condemn her to an asylum, Louise Michel fled to London in July 1890 and lived in exile for the next five years.

London and Paris

At the end of the 19th century, the British capital was home to many exiled European radicals and anarchists. In London, Louise opened the International School for the children of political refugees — probably the first libertarian school to be founded in Britain. The flavor of the school is suggested by the membership of the school board, which included the English designer and socialist William Morris, the Russian anarchist Prince Peter Kropotkin and Italian revolutionary Errico Malatesta. The school prospectus included a statement by the Russian anarchist Mikhail Bakunin:

> All rational education is at bottom nothing but the progressive immolation of authority for the benefit of liberty, the final object of education necessarily being the formation of free men full of respect and love for the liberty of others.

The school promoted "rational and integral education": no subjects were compulsory, teaching was in small groups and students were encouraged to think for themselves. However, the school was closed in 1892 after the police claimed they had found bomb-making equipment in the basement.

On November 13, 1895, Michel returned to Paris to a massive welcome rally at Saint-Lazare station, and resumed her speaking tours around France in support of anarchist and workers' causes. For the next 10 years, ignoring poor health, she continued to travel between London, Paris, Edinburgh and other European capitals to preach the gospel of rebellion.

Traveling anarchist

Although widely respected, as a woman she did not command the same authority in revolutionary circles as leaders like Blanqui, Kropotkin and Marx. But Michel continued to play a significant role in the debates of the late 19th century between anarchists, socialists and communists over the best way to create revolution.

In July 1881, Louise Michel attended the International Congress of Workers and Syndicalists in Britain. The meeting was organized by the anarchist leader Peter Kropotkin, who hoped to create an anarchist "Black International" to match Karl Marx's communist First International. Michel traveled to London as a representative of French anarchist groups, joining delegates from Europe, the United States, Mexico, Russia and beyond. The congress, however, was a failure, and a second attempt — the Second International Congress of 1896 — saw a lasting rupture between Marxist social democrats and anarchists.

After being arrested in Belgium and expelled from the country in September 1897, Michel continued to travel between Paris and London from 1898 to 1900, attending conferences and editing her writings on the Paris Commune.

In exile, she played a public role in supporting trade unionists, anarchists and democrats facing police repression. Police archives record her speaking at Nelson's Column in Trafalgar Square in support of radicals imprisoned and tortured in Spain. She campaigned in London alongside British labor leader Tom Mann, and anarchists Kropotkin, Malatesta and Emma Goldman in support of the Haymarket martyrs (executed after a bomb killed policemen in Chicago, United States, at a protest for the eight-hour day on May 1, 1886). In December 1899, Michel appeared again in London with Goldman and Kropotkin, at a "Grand Meeting and Concert for the

Benefit of the Agitation in Favor of the Political Victims in Italy." She also condemned the anti-Semitism of the right, as she followed the campaign for Captain Alfred Dreyfus, a French Army officer falsely accused of treason and jailed on the penal colony of Devil's Island.

Stricken with pneumonia at age 71, she nearly died, but returned to France from London on May 15, 1902, to continue a series of public meetings.

Throughout 1903, she toured France with the young anarchist journalist Ernest Girault, until she returned to London on October 27, 1903, ill once again. A second tour of public meetings with Girault starting in February 1904 was cut short in Toulon on March 20 because of her ill health. In May, Louise drafted her will, leaving her few possessions to her comrade Charlotte Vauvelle, and asking to be buried beside her mother, without religious ceremony, at the Levallois-Perret cemetery. That month, she started her speaking tours again, but the toll on her health was too great.

After visiting Algeria in late 1904, she arrived exhausted in the southern French city of Marseilles — where she died on January 9, 1905, aged 74.

Posters throughout the capital announced: "People of Paris, Louise Michel is dead." The Paris Police Commissioner mobilized nearly 10,000 police for her funeral. Her coffin was transported from Marseilles to Paris and on January 22, 1905, a procession of 120,000 people followed her coffin from the Gare de Lyon station in Paris to the Levallois-Perret cemetery.

That day, the czar's troops fired on demonstrators in front of the Winter Palace in St. Petersburg, Russia — the precursor to the Russian Revolution. Louise Michel's legacy lives on.

Nic Maclellan
Melbourne, Australia
March 2004

Viro Major

Having seen the immense massacre, the combat
the people on their cross, Paris on its pallet bed,
Tremendous pity was in your words.
You did what the great mad souls do
And, weary of fighting, dreaming, suffering,
You said, "I killed!" because you wanted to die.

You lied against yourself, terrible and superhuman.
Judith the sombre Jewess, Aria the Roman
Would have clapped their hands while you spoke.
You said to the lofts: "I burnt the palaces!"
You glorified those who are crushed and downtrodden.
You cried: "I killed! Let them kill me!" — And the crowd
Listened to this haughty woman accuse herself.
You seemed to blow a kiss to the sepulchre;
Your steady gaze weighed on the livid judges:
And you dreamed, like the grave Eumenides.

Pale death stood behind you.
The vast hall was full of terror.
Because the bleeding people detest civil war.
Outside could be heard the sound of the town.
This woman listened to the noisy life
From above, in an austere attitude of refusal.
She did not seem to understand anything other than
A pillory erected for a finale:
And, finding affront noble and agony beautiful,
Sinister, she hastened her steps toward the tomb.
The judges murmured: "Let her die! It is fair.
She is vile — at least she is not majestic,"
Said their conscience. And the judges, pensive,

Facing yes, facing no, as between two reefs,
Hesitated, watching the severe culprit.

And those who, like me, know you to be incapable
Of all that is not heroism and virtue,
Who know if they asked you, "Where are you from?"
That you would reply, "I come from the night where there is
      suffering;
Yes, I come from the duty which you have made an abyss!"
Those who know your mysterious and sweet verses,
Your days, your nights, your cares, your tears given to all.
Your forgetting of yourself to aid others
Your words which resemble the flames of the apostles;
Those who know the roof without fire, without air, without
      bread
The bed of webbing with the fir table
Your goodness, your pride as a woman of the people.
The acrid emotion which sleeps beneath your anger.

Your long look of hate at all the inhuman people
And the feet of the children warmed by your hands:
Those people, woman, facing your timid majesty
Meditated, and despite the bitter fold of your mouth
Despite the one who cursed and hounded you
Who hurled at you the undignified cries of the law
Despite your high, fatal voice with which you accused yourself
They saw the angel's splendor beyond the medusa.

You were tall, and seemed strange in these debates:
For, puny like those who live down there,
Nothing bothers them more than two conflicting souls,
Than the divine chaos of starry things
Seen at the depths of a great inclement heart,
Than the radiation seen in a blaze.

December 18, 1871
(Trans. —Jodie Martire)

chapter one: *Early Life*

Growing up in the northeastern region of Haute-Marne, Louise Michel's radical vision grew out of her experiences in the countryside. In her Memoirs, *written in prison in the 1880s, she looks back on her youth, considering her anger at the mistreatment of animals and rural peasants as sources of her rebellion.*

When she moved to Paris in the early 1850s, Louise Michel began to meet more of the impoverished members of the city. In her poetry, she started to record her pity for the underclass, and her anger at the wealthy.

Louise Michel
Sources of rebellion

Above everything else, I am taken by the revolution. It had to be that way. The wind that blew through the ruin where I was born, the old people who brought me up, the solitude and freedom of my childhood, the legends of the Haute-Marne, the scraps of knowledge gleaned from here and there — all that opened my ear to every harmony, my spirit to every illumination, my heart to both love and hate. Everything intermingled in a single song, a single dream, a single love: the revolution.

As far back as I can remember, the origin of my revolt against the powerful was my horror at the tortures inflicted on animals. I used to wish animals could get revenge, that the dog could bite the man who was mercilessly beating him, that the horse bleeding under the whip could throw off the man tormenting him. But mute animals always submit to their fate…

Animals always submit, and the more ferocious a man is toward animals, the more that man cringes before the people who dominate him…

My evenings in the village added to the feeling of revolt that I have felt time and time again. The peasants sow and harvest the grain, but they do not always have bread. One woman told me how during a bad year — that is what they call a year when the monopolists starve the country — neither she, nor her husband, nor their four children were able to eat every day. Owning only the clothes on their backs, they had nothing more to sell. Merchants who had grain gave them no more credit, not even a few oats to make a little bread, and two of their children died, they believed, from hunger.

"You have to submit," she said to me. "Everybody can't eat bread every day."

Her husband had wanted to kill the man who had refused them credit at 100 percent interest while their children were dying, but she stopped him. The two children who managed to survive ultimately went to work for the man whom her husband wanted to kill. The usurer gave them hardly any wages, but poor people, she said, "should submit to that which they cannot prevent."

Her manner was calm when she told me that story. I had gone hot-eyed with rage, and I said to her, "You should have let your husband do what he wanted to do. He was right."

I could imagine the poor little ones dying of hunger. She had made that picture of misery so distressing that I could feel it myself. I saw the husband in his torn shirt, his wooden shoes chafing his bare feet, going to beg at the evil usurer's and returning sadly over the frozen roads with nothing. I saw him shaking his fists threateningly when his little ones were lying dead on a handful of straw. I saw his wife stopping him from avenging his own children and others. I saw the two surviving children growing up with this memory, and then going off to work for that man: the cowards.

I thought that if that usurer had come into the village at that moment I would have leaped at his throat to bite it, and I told her that. I was indignant at her believing everybody couldn't have food every day. Such stupidity bewildered me. "You mustn't talk like that, little one," the woman said. "It makes God cry."

Have you ever seen sheep lift their throats to the knife? That woman had the mind of a ewe…

Something more than charity was necessary if each person was always to have something to eat. As for the rich, I had little respect for them. I know the full reality of heavy work on the land. I know the woes of the peasant. He is incessantly bent over land that is as harsh as a stepmother. For his labor all he gets is leftovers from his master, and he can get even less comfort from thought and dreams than we can. Heavy work bends both men and oxen over the furrows, keeping the slaughterhouse for worn-out beasts and the beggar's sack for worn-out humans.

The land. That word is at the very bottom of my life. It was in the thick, illustrated Roman history from which my whole family on both sides had learned how to read. My grandmother had taught me to read from it, pointing out the letters with her large knitting needle. Reared in the country, I understood the agrarian revolts of old Rome, and I shed many tears on the pages of that book. The death of the Greeks oppressed me then as much as the gallows of Russia did later.

How misleading are these texts about the happiness of the fields. The descriptions of nature are true, but the description of the happiness of workers in the fields is a lie. People who know no better gaze at the flowers of the fields and the beautiful fresh grass and believe that the children who watch over the livestock play there. The little ones want grass only to stretch out in and sleep a little at noon. The shadow of the woods, the yellowing crops that the wind moves like waves — the peasant is too tired to find them beautiful.

His work is heavy, his day is long but he resigns himself, he always resigns himself, for his will is broken. Man is overworked like a beast. He is half dead and works for his exploiter without thinking. No peasants get rich by working the land; they only make money for people who already have too much. Many men have told me, in words that echoed what the woman told me at the village: "You must not say that, little one. It offends God." That's what they said to me when I told them that everyone has a right to everything there is on earth.

My pity for everything that suffers went far — more perhaps for the silent beast than for man. My revolt against social inequalities went further. It grew, and it has continued to grow, through the battles and across the carnage. It dominates my grief, and it dominates my life. There was no way that I could have stopped myself from throwing my life to the revolution.

From: *The Red Virgin — Memoirs of Louise Michel.*

Louise Michel
Poem

I have seen criminals and whores
And spoken with them. Now I inquire
If you believe them, made as now they are
To drag their rags in blood and mire
Preordained, an evil race?

You to whom all men are prey
Have made them what they are today.

Louise Michel
Letter to Victor Hugo

In 1851, Louise Michel traveled briefly to Paris with her mother. During this visit, she met the famous writer Victor Hugo, author of The Hunchback of Notre Dame *and* Les Misérables, *forming a lifetime friendship. On her return to the province of Haute-Marne, she sent him numerous poems and letters.*

Yesterday I left the old chateau at Vroncourt, maybe never to see it again. At present, I'm far from my mother and in a small boarding school where I'm preparing to take an examination in August which will allow me to teach.

Courage often fails me. I want to confess to you, brother, you who understands all the tortures facing a small child, with all affection and illusions shattered. All my life is passing before my eyes as if in a dream, and I dare not look toward the future.

Allow me to open my soul to you. You are good and great like God — Hugo, please give me a word of hope and maybe I will believe again in good fortune…

My thoughts drift in the gloom, and I need a powerful voice to say: "Let there be light!" and cast away these shadows. Write me a few lines, so that I can find some courage again, as my strength comes from God and from you, brother…

Louise Michel,

Madame Beth's Boarding School
Chaumont en Bassigny,
Haute-Marne, 1851.

> Xavière Gauthier (ed), *Louise Michel,*
> *je vous écris de ma nuit.* (Trans. —*Ed.*)

chapter two: *Seizing the Guns*

The famous incident that sparked the Paris Commune was an attempt by the conservative government in Versailles to seize the cannon held by the republican National Guard in Paris. Before dawn on March 18, 1871, the Versailles Government sent 4,000 troops to seize the guns. Louise Michel's Memoirs tell how she helped rally women to stop the troops from dragging them away.

These events were dramatized in the last full-length play written by famous German playwright Bertolt Brecht. As an anti-Nazi refugee living in the United States, Brecht was named as a subversive after World War II. After giving evidence to the House Un-American Activities Committee, where he denied being a member of the U.S. Communist Party, he left the United States for East Germany. In 1949, Brecht founded the Berliner Ensemble, which became the country's foremost theater company. He wrote only one new play before his death in 1956: Die Tage der Commune (The Days of the Commune).

Louise Michel
Seizing the guns

Faced with surrender to the Prussian Army, the Commune and popular associations mobilized to take power on March 18, 1871.

The cannon paid for by the National Guard had been left on some vacant land in the middle of the zone abandoned by the Prussians. Paris objected to that, and the cannon were taken to the Parc Wagram. The idea was in the air that each battalion should recapture its own cannon. A battalion of the National Guard from the sixth arrondissement gave us our impetus. With the flag in front, men and women and children hauled the cannon by hand down the boulevards, and although the cannon were loaded, no accidents occurred. Montmartre, like Belleville and Batignolles, had its own cannon. Those that had been placed in the Place des Vosges were moved to the faubourg Saint Antoine. Some sailors proposed our recapturing the Prussian-occupied forts around the city by boarding them like ships, and this idea intoxicated us.

Then before dawn on March 18, the Versailles reactionaries sent in troops to seize the cannon now held by the National Guard. One of the points they moved toward was the Butte of Montmartre, where our cannon had been taken. The soldiers of the reactionaries captured our artillery by surprise, but they were unable to haul them away as they had intended, because they had neglected to bring horses with them.

Learning that the Versailles soldiers were trying to seize the cannon, men and women of Montmartre swarmed up the Butte in a surprise maneuver. Those people who were climbing believed they would die, but they were prepared to pay the price.

The Butte of Montmartre was bathed in the first light of day, through which things were glimpsed as if they were hidden behind a thin veil of water. Gradually the crowd increased. The other districts of Paris, hearing of the events taking place on the Butte of Montmartre, came to our assistance.

The women of Paris covered the cannon with their bodies. When their officers ordered the soldiers to fire, the men refused. The same army that would be used to crush Paris two months later decided now that it did not want to be an accomplice of the reaction. They gave up their attempt to seize the cannon from the National Guard. They understood that the people were defending the republic by defending the arms that the royalists and imperialists would have turned on Paris in agreement with the Prussians. When we had won our victory, I looked around and noticed my poor mother, who had followed me to the Butte of Montmartre, believing that I was going to die.

On this day, March 18, the people wakened. If they had not, it would have been the triumph of some king; instead it was a triumph of the people. March 18 could have belonged to the allies of kings, or to foreigners, or to the people. It was the people's...

From: Louise Michel, *Mémoires*. (Trans. —*Ed.*)

Louise Michel
Open letter defending the seizing of the guns in Montmartre

After Louise Michel led the women of Montmartre to protect cannon deployed on the hill overlooking Paris, Versailles leader Adolphe Thiers told the newspapers that the cannon belong to the state and not the people. Louise Michel wrote an open letter in protest.

Protest from the citizens of Montmartre:

Will we be betrayed in the end? No, Montmartre has not asked to be disarmed!

Our fathers, brothers, husbands are as indignant as we are reading these things in the papers. But if the men were to give back these cannon placed on the Butte of Montmartre to defend the republic, we women citizens would defend them to the death, just as we will defend to the last ramparts the violated honor of our nation which has been betrayed.

Long live the republic!
For the citizens of Montmartre,
The secretary, Louise Michel.

Xavière Gauthier (ed), *Louise Michel, je vous écris de ma nuit.* (Trans. —*Ed.*)

Bertolt Brecht
The Days of the Commune

Montmartre, March 18, 1871

Six o'clock in the morning. It is getting light. The blinds of the bakery are raised. A window shutter is opened. In some houses lights are switched on. Two women cross the square. Before they enter the shop they see the soldiers around the gun.

1st WOMAN: What does he think he's doing with the gun?

4th WOMAN: That's Phillippe. He used to work in the baker's here. You've come back just in time, Phillippe. The bakery opened up again yesterday.

PHILLIPPE: Take it easy, I haven't come to visit the boss.

1st WOMAN: What are all that lot doing with him?

4th WOMAN: He's led them here because he knows the district.

1st WOMAN: What are you trying to do with that gun?

PHILLIPPE: Clear off. It's none of your business. We're taking it to Versailles. By order.

1st WOMAN: You wouldn't dare. You wouldn't dare lay a hand on that gun, you shitehawk.

PHILLIPPE: Come on ladies, less of it. Clear off.

1st WOMAN: Jean Cabet!

4th WOMAN: Jean!

1st WOMAN: They're trying to pinch the gun.

PHILLIPPE: Shut up. You'll wake up the whole street.

4th and 1st WOMEN: Jean, Jean, they're trying to run off with the gun!!

PHILLIPPE: That's dropped us right in it. Where's the bloody horses?

Jean runs from the house in trousers and shirt.
JEAN: What's the matter? (*Two soldiers grab him.*)

He recognizes Phillippe and calls to the house.
JEAN: François, your brother's working for Thiers.

François comes out of the house putting his spectacles on.
JEAN: They're trying to snatch the gun.
FRANÇOIS: You leave the gun alone. It doesn't belong to you.
PHILLIPPE (*laughing*): Since when were you in the National Guard?
FRANÇOIS: The seminary shut down. Keep your thieving hands off that gun.

François is jumped by the other soldiers.
FRANÇOIS: Get off me.
PHILLIPPE: Take it easy kidder.
JEAN: Somebody run and beat the drums.
PHILLIPPE: You're wasting your time. We slashed the drums as a precaution.
FRANÇOIS: They've covered the whole district.
PHILLIPPE: Shhuussh.
1st SOLDIER: Shut up.
FRANÇOIS: The church bells.
JEAN: You bastards.

(He breaks away and gets clear of the soldiers. One aims his rifle at him.)
PHILLIPPE: Don't shoot, or we'll have the whole lot of them down on top of us.
1st SOLDIER: If the horses don't come in a minute we'll be sunk in any case.

The women return. By and by the square fills up with women. They block the exits. One woman goes up to the soldiers with a piece of bread and offers it. The 2nd soldier takes it.

2nd SOLDIER: I wish they'd get a bloody move on with their horses.

5th WOMAN: We've got white bread here. All you get with Thiers is bellyache.

GENEVIEVE: We got this bread from Thiers. He robbed you to pay us, so you can take it with a clear conscience.

2nd WOMAN: Now I can see why we got the white bread. He wants a straight swap. Guns for bread. He must think we're daft.

5th WOMAN: Where're you from son?

2nd SOLDIER: From the Auvergne.

5th WOMAN: Ah, from the Auvergne. A farm yacker?

GENEVIEVE: A peasant.

BABETTE: I bet they sent you here without your breakfast, didn't they?

1st SOLDIER: They didn't think we'd be out long.

BABETTE: We got the white bread and you go hungry.

1st WOMAN: Have a sup of this, lad. Now then, what is there around here that could interest a young lad like you?

3rd SOLDIER: Eh! Don't tear us to bits. Leave us in one piece.

PHILLIPPE: Now come on ladies, you are hindering me in the execution of my duty.

GENEVIEVE: Get inside François. We can handle this without bloodshed.

FRANÇOIS: Be careful, Genevieve.

3rd SOLDIER: The war's over. All we want to do is go home.

5th WOMAN: Come home with me.

2nd SOLDIER: This is seeding time, but you don't think of this do you — you town people.

4th WOMAN: They ought to be ashamed of themselves, setting on women and then dodging their duty!

6th WOMAN: Look at them shivering. The only thing they'll get stiff with is cold. Come over here lad, a bit closer to the fire.

5th WOMAN: There are better games to play than soldiers.

1st WOMAN: Let's stop the fighting. How good are you at drilling?

Stand to attention. Right. To the front salute.

PHILLIPPE: Quiet, quiet, quiet.

OFFICER *(from the rear)*: The horse teams can't get through. The guns will have to be manhandled. Anyone who resists is to be shot out of hand. That's an order from General Lecomte.

PHILLIPPE: Go on, pick up the traces. *(To the women.)* Shift.

6th WOMAN: Are you going to fight against us just because your lousy general tells you to?

PHILLIPPE: Shove off.

GENEVIEVE: You won't take the guns away, you wretches. We'll throw ourselves under the wheels.

PHILLIPPE: The first one who gets in the way will be shot.

The soldiers struggle to inch the gun forward.

6th WOMAN: Are you going to massacre the lot of us?

Genevieve throws herself in *front of the gun.*

BABETTE: Genevieve!

PHILLIPPE *(to the women)*: Get away or I'll fire.

François comes out of the house with a rifle.

FRANÇOIS: Get out of the road, Phillippe.

PHILLIPPE: Give me that rifle kidder.

BABETTE: Shoot him down. *(She repeats this three or four times.)*

GENEVIEVE *(steps between them)*: No bloodshed.

BABETTE: Keep out of it Genevieve.

PHILLIPPE *(aiming)*: Drop that gun, kid.

FRANÇOIS: You make one move and I'll shoot. Our Father, which art in Heaven, hallowed be Thy name…

6th WOMAN: What's this baker's boy? Are you going to shoot down your own brother because General Lecomte tells you to.

5th WOMAN: Cain!

PHILLIPPE: I'm going to count up to three. One…

GENEVIEVE: François, don't shoot. We are in the right.

FRANÇOIS: Thy kingdom come, Thy will be done, on earth as it is

in Heaven. *(Getting louder.)* Give us this day our daily bread...
PHILLIPPE: Two...
FRANÇOIS: And forgive us our trespasses...

The window opens and Mme Cabet looks out.
MME CABET: Phillippe, put that rifle down at once. How can you
think of such things. Shooting your own brother and him a student
of physics. The government wants peace and order... I stick to it
and you can damn well do the same. But then you can't even read,
I don't suppose you even know what the government wants.
BAKER'S WIFE: Yes, Madame Cabet, peace and order. An end to
all this shooting. Let's get rid of the gun.
1st WOMAN: It's our gun.
BAKER'S WIFE: That's not true. The gun belongs to the National
Guard, damn them for heathen troublemakers. Isn't that so?
Phillippe, if you don't get that gun away from here I'm not having
you back in my bakery. So get on with it.

*Mme Cabet shuts the window, she comes down stairs. Phillippe gets
his men working on the gun. Mme Cabet leaves the house, pushes
the soldiers off the gun and puts her hand on it.*
MME CABET: The gun belongs to me.
BAKER'S WIFE: What?
GENEVIEVE: It's true. Madame Cabet raised the money for it. But
you, Madame Poulard never gave a sou. *(To the soldiers.)* The gun
belongs to Madame Cabet just as her pots and pans do. You can't
have it.
PHILLIPPE: Oh come on. Let's talk sense.
BAKER'S WIFE: This is treachery.
BABETTE: Paying back treachery in its own coin.
BAKER'S WIFE: You're sacked.

Laughter. The door shuts.
1st WOMAN: You can stuff your mouldy bread.
5th WOMAN: They can't expect you to shoot your own brother.

PHILLIPPE: I'm not a baker and I'm not a brother, ladies, I'm doing my duty.

GENEVIEVE *(to the other soldiers)*: And the rest of you…? What are you going to do with your guns?

2nd SOLDIER: Shit, we shouldn't have to do this…

Around the gun upon which Mme Cabet is sitting a thick crowd has collected, Papa and Coco come running with fixed bayonets. Noise comes from everywhere.

PAPA: Get away from the gun.

MME CABET: Good morning.

PAPA: Morning.

COCO: Morning.

BABETTE: This is Madame Cabet's gun.

PAPA: So I see.

COCO: I can hardly believe it.

PAPA: Long live Madame Cabet, sole owner of the gun in the Rue Pigalle. What's up with him?

PHILLIPPE: It's not our fault they didn't send us horses. We can't push our way through these women.

Laughter from the women.

PAPA: You see, fine words. Turn bayonets. Hold onto them. Take them to your hearts where they can't do any harm.

Langevin enters.

BABETTE: Uncle Pierre.

PAPA: Where have you come from?

LANGEVIN *(confidentially)*: Straight from General Lecomte. He gave the order for two of us to be shot in the Rue Lepic, but his men turned on him and arrested him. I've been released and I came straight here.

PAPA: Lecomte. We know all about that pig. He's got to answer for the January killings. Where is he now?

LANGEVIN: They took him to the guard post.

PAPA: We've got to get there quick. If he isn't in our hands in five minutes they'll let him escape.

COCO: Calm down Papa.

PAPA: Calm down… Me. This is a matter of life and death and you tell me to calm down…

LANGEVIN: The Central Committee will be meeting this evening.

GENEVIEVE: We won't pay back killing with killing.

PAPA: No Mademoiselle, we'll let them slaughter us like we did in January. *(He rushes off.)*

LANGEVIN: The general will be tried in a court of law, brother.

PAPA: We are the law.

LANGEVIN: Let's barricade the streets. They might attack us at any time.

MME CABET: Perhaps someone will give me a hand down?

From: Bertolt Brecht, *The Days of the Commune*
(London: Eyre Metheun, 1978).

chapter three: *Paris Enraged*

Following the failure of Versailles to seize the guns defending Paris, elections were held for a new administration in the city of Paris. In later years, the Paris Commune served as a model for socialists and radicals across Europe.

On the 20th anniversary of the crushing of the Commune, Karl Marx's collaborator Friedrich Engels wrote about the history of the Commune.

From September 1870, Paris was besieged by Prussian troops. During the winter of 1870, there was increasing starvation and hardship among working people in the capital. In her Memoirs, *Louise Michel describes her participation in the creation of local associations in the working-class suburb of Montmartre, and her role in the defense of the Commune.*

Friedrich Engels
History of the Commune

The necessary consequence was the Paris Revolution of September 4, 1870. The empire collapsed like a house of cards, and the republic was again proclaimed. But the enemy was standing at the gates; the armies of the empire were either hopelessly encircled at Metz or held captive in Germany. In this emergency the people allowed the Paris deputies to the former legislative body to constitute themselves into a "Government of National Defense." This was the more readily conceded, since, for the purposes of defense, all Parisians capable of bearing arms had enrolled in the National Guard and were armed, so that now the workers constituted a great majority. But very soon the antagonism between the almost completely bourgeois government and the armed proletariat broke into open conflict. On October 31, workers' battalions stormed the town hall and captured part of the membership of the government. Treachery, the government's direct breach of its undertakings, and the intervention of some petty-bourgeois battalions set them free again, and in order not to occasion the outbreak of civil war inside a city besieged by a foreign military power, the former government was left in office.

At last, on January 28, 1871, starved Paris capitulated. But with honors unprecedented in the history of war. The forts were surrendered, the city wall stripped of guns, the weapons of the regiments of the line and of the Mobile Guard were handed over, and they themselves considered prisoners of war. But the National Guard kept its weapons and guns, and only entered into an armistice with the victors. And these did not dare enter Paris in triumph. They only dared to occupy a tiny corner of Paris, which, into the bargain, consisted partly of public parks, and even this they only occupied for a few days! And during this time they, who had maintained their encirclement of Paris for 131 days, were themselves encircled by the armed workers of Paris, who kept a sharp watch that no "Prussian" should overstep the narrow bounds of the corner ceded to the foreign conqueror. Such was the respect which the Paris workers inspired in the army before which all the armies of the empire had laid down their arms; and the Prussian Junkers, who had come to take revenge at the home of the revolution, were compelled to stand by respectfully, and salute precisely this armed revolution!

During the war the Paris workers had confined themselves to demanding the vigorous prosecution of the fight. But now, when peace had come after the capitulation of Paris, now Thiers, the new supreme head of the government, was compelled to realize that the rule of the propertied classes — big landowners and capitalists — was in constant danger so long as the workers of Paris had arms in their hands. His first action was an attempt to disarm them. On March 18, he sent troops of the line with orders to rob the National Guard of the artillery belonging to it, which had been constructed during the siege of Paris and had been paid for by public subscription. The attempt failed; Paris mobilized as one man for resistance, and war between Paris and the French Government sitting at Versailles was declared. On March 26 the Paris Commune was elected and on March 28 it was proclaimed. The Central Committee of the National Guard, which up to then had carried on the government, handed in its resignation to the Commune after it had first decreed the abolition of the scandalous Paris "Morality Police." On March 30, the Commune abolished conscription and the standing army, and declared the sole armed force to be the National Guard, in which all citizens capable of bearing arms were to be enrolled. It remitted all payments of rent for dwelling houses from October 1870 until April, the amounts already paid to be booked as future rent payments, and stopped all sales of articles pledged in the municipal loan office. On the same day the foreigners elected to the Commune were confirmed in office, because "the flag of the Commune is the flag of the World Republic." On April 1, it was decided that the highest salary to be received by any employee of the Commune, and therefore also by its members themselves, was not to exceed 6,000 francs (4,800 marks). On the following day the Commune decreed the separation of the church from the state, and the abolition of all state payments for religious purposes as well as the transformation of all church property into national property; as a result of which, on April 8, the exclusion from the schools of all religious symbols, pictures, dogmas, prayers — in a word, "of all that belongs to the sphere of the individual's conscience" — was ordered and gradually put into effect.

On April 5, in reply to the shooting, day after day, of captured Commune fighters by the Versailles troops, a decree was issued for the imprisonment of hostages, but it was never carried into execution. On April 6, the guillotine was brought out by the 137th battalion of the National Guard, and publicly burnt, amid great popular rejoicing. On April 12, the Commune decided that the Victory Column on the Place Vendôme, which had been cast from captured guns by Napoleon after the war of 1809, should be demolished as a symbol of chauvinism and incitement to national hatred. This was carried out on May 16. On April 16, it ordered a statistical tabulation of factories which had been closed down by the manufacturers, and the working out of plans for the operation of these factories by the workers formerly employed in them, who were to be organized in cooperative societies, and also plans for the organization of these cooperatives into one great union. On April 20, it abolished night work for bakers, and also the employment offices, which since the Second Empire had been run as a monopoly by creatures appointed by the police-labor exploiters of the first rank; these offices were transferred to the mayoralties of the 20 arrondissements of Paris. On April 30, it ordered the closing of the pawnshops, on the ground that they were a private exploitation of the workers, and were in contradiction with the right of the workers to their instruments of labor and to credit. On May 5, it ordered the razing of the Chapel of Atonement, which had been built in expiation of the execution of Louis XVI.

Thus from March 18 onwards the class character of the Paris movement, which had previously been pushed into the background by the fight against the foreign invaders, emerged sharply and clearly. As almost only workers, or recognized representatives of the workers, sat in the Commune, its decisions bore a decidedly proletarian character. Either these decisions decreed reforms which the republican bourgeoisie had failed to pass solely out of cowardice, but which provided a necessary basis for the free activity of the working class — such as the realization of the principle that *in relation to the state,* religion is a purely private matter — or the Commune promulgated decrees which were in the direct interest of the working class and in part cut deeply into the old order of society. In a beleaguered city, however, it was possible to make at most a start in the realization of all this. And from the beginning of May onwards all their energies were taken up by the fight against the armies assembled by the Versailles Government in ever-growing numbers.

On April 7, the Versailles troops had captured the Seine crossing at Neuilly, on the western front of Paris; on the other hand, in an attack on the southern front on April 11 they were repulsed with heavy losses by General Eudes. Paris was continually bombarded and, moreover, by the very people who had stigmatized as a sacrilege the bombardment of the same city by the Prussians. These same people now begged the Prussian Government for the hasty return of the French soldiers taken prisoner at Sedan and Metz, in order that they might recapture Paris for them. From the beginning of May the gradual arrival of these troops gave the Versailles forces a decided superiority. This already became evident when, on April 23, Thiers broke off the negotiations for the exchange, proposed by the Commune of the Archbishop of Paris and a whole number of other priests held as hostages in Paris, for only one man, Blanqui, who had twice been elected to the Commune but was a prisoner in

Clairvaux. And even more from the changed language of Thiers; previously procrastinating and equivocal, he now suddenly became insolent, threatening, brutal.

The Versailles forces took the redoubt of Moulin Saquet on the southern front on May 3; on May 9, Fort Issy, which had been completely reduced to ruins by gunfire; on May 14, Fort Vanves. On the western front they advanced gradually, capturing the numerous villages and buildings which extended up to the city wall, until they reached the main defenses; on May 21, thanks to treachery and the carelessness of the National Guards stationed there, they succeeded in forcing their way into the city. The Prussians, who held the northern and eastern forts, allowed the Versailles troops to advance across the land north of the city, which was forbidden ground to them under the armistice, and thus to march forward, attacking on a wide front, which the Parisians naturally thought covered by the armistice, and therefore held only weakly. As a result of this, only a weak resistance was put up in the western half of Paris, in the luxury city proper; it grew stronger and more tenacious the nearer the incoming troops approached the eastern half, the working-class city proper.

It was only after eight days' fighting that the last defenders of the Commune succumbed on the heights of Belleville and Menilmontant; and then the massacre of defenseless men, women and children, which had been raging all through the week on an increasing scale, reached its zenith. The breechloaders could no longer kill fast enough; the vanquished were shot down in hundreds by *mitrailleuse* fire. The "Wall of the Federals" at the Père Lachaise cemetery, where the final mass murder was consummated, is still standing today, a mute but eloquent testimony to the frenzy of which the ruling class is capable as soon as the working class dares to stand up for its rights. Then, when the slaughter of them all proved to be impossible, came the mass arrests, the shooting of victims arbitrarily selected from the prisoners' ranks, and the removal of the rest to great camps where they awaited trial by courts-martial. The Prussian troops surrounding the northeastern half of Paris had orders not to allow any fugitives to pass; but the officers often shut their eyes when the soldiers paid more obedience to the dictates of humanity than to those of the Supreme Command; particular honor is due to the Saxon army corps, which behaved very humanely and let through many who were obviously fighters for the Commune.

From: Friedrich Engels, "Introduction" to *The Civil War in France*.

Louise Michel
Life during the Commune

In Montmartre, in the 18th arrondissement, we organized the Montmartre Vigilance Committee. Few of its members still survive, but during the siege the committee made the reactionaries tremble. Every evening, we would burst out onto the streets from our headquarters, sometimes simply to talk up the revolution, because the time for duplicity had passed. We knew how little the reactionary regime, in its death throes, valued its promises and the lives of its citizens, and the people had to be warned.

Actually there were two vigilance committees in Montmartre, the men's and the women's. Although I presided over the women's committee, I was always at the men's, because its members included some Russian revolutionaries.

I still have an old map of Paris that hung on the wall of our meeting room. I carried it back and forth across the ocean with me as a souvenir. With ink we had blotted out the empire's coat of arms, which desecrated it and which would have dirtied our headquarters.

The members of the men's Montmartre Vigilance Committee were remarkable persons. Never have I seen minds so direct, so unpretentious, and so elevated. Never have I seen individuals so clearheaded. I don't know how this group managed to do it. There were no weaknesses. Something good and strong supported people.

The women were courageous also, and among them, too, there were some remarkable minds. I belonged to both committees, and the leanings of the two groups were the same. Sometime in the future, the women's committee should have its own history told. Or perhaps the two should be mingled, because people didn't worry about which sex they were before they did their duty. That stupid question was settled.

In the evenings I often was able to be at meetings of both groups, since the women's, which met at the office of the justice of the peace on the Rue de la Chapelle, began an hour earlier than the men's. Thus after the women's meeting was over I could go to the last half of the men's meeting, and sometimes other women and I could go to the entire men's meeting.

The Montmartre Vigilance Committees left no one without shelter and no one without food. Anyone could eat at the meeting hall, although as the siege continued and food supplies became shorter, it might only be one herring divided between five or six people. For people who were really in need we didn't hesitate to dip into our resources or to use revolutionary requisitioning. The 18th arrondissement was the terror of profiteers. When the reactionaries heard the phrase "Montmartre is going to come down on you," they hid in their holes. We chased them down anyway, and like hunted beasts they fled, leaving behind the hiding places where provisions were rotting while Paris starved.

Ultimately the Montmartre Vigilance Committees were mowed down, like all revolutionary groups. The rare members still alive know how proud we were there and how fervently we flew the flag of the revolution. Little did it matter to those who were there whether they were beaten to the ground unnoticed in battle or died alone in the sunlight. It makes no difference how the millstone moves so long as the bread is made.

With the weakness of the French Army, the people's militia, called the National Guard, took on greater importance in the defense of Paris. Prussian troops advanced through France to the gates of the French capital.

The Prussian siege continued; the days became dark and the trees lost their leaves. Hunger and cold reached more deeply into the houses of Paris.

On October 31, at the Hôtel de Ville, the people proclaimed the

Commune. The Committees of Vigilance from all over Paris organized the demonstration, and the people no longer cried out "Long live the republic." They cried out "Long live the Commune!"

Another month went by and conditions became increasingly bad. The National Guard could have saved the city, but the Government of National Defense feared supporting the armed force of the people.

Early in December, I was arrested a second time. That second arrest came when several women who had more courage than fore-sight wanted to propose some unknown means of defense to the government. Their zeal was so great that they came to the Women's Vigilance Committee in Montmartre... We agreed to join them the next day in a demonstration in front of the Hôtel de Ville, but we made one reservation. We told them we would go as women to share their danger; we would not go as citizens because we no longer recognized the Government of National Defense. It had proved itself incapable even of letting Paris defend itself.

The next day we went to the rendezvous at the Hôtel de Ville, and we expected what happened: I was arrested for having organ-ized the demonstration. I answered their charges by saying that I couldn't have organized any demonstration to speak to the govern-ment, because I no longer recognized that government. I added that when I came on my own behalf to the Hôtel de Ville, it would be with an armed uprising behind me. That explanation appeared unsatisfactory to them, and they locked me up.

The next day four citizens came to claim me "in the name of the 18th arrondissement." At this declaration, the reactionaries became frightened. "Montmartre is going to descend on us," they whispered to each other, and they released me.

It wasn't until January 19, when the struggle was almost over, that the Government of National Defense finally agreed to let the National Guard effect a sortie to try to retake Montretout and Buzen-val. At first the National Guard swept the Prussians before them, but the mud defeated the brave sons of the people. They sank into the wet earth up to their ankles, and unable to get their artillery up on the hills, they had to retreat. Hundreds stayed behind, lying quietly in death; these men of the National Guard — men of the people, artists, young persons — died with no regrets for their lost lives. The earth drank the blood of this first Parisian carnage; soon it would drink more.

Paris still did not wish to surrender to the Prussians. On January 22, the people gathered in front of the Hôtel de Ville, where General Chaudey, who commanded the soldiers, now had his headquarters. The people sensed that the members of the government were lying when they declared they were not thinking of surrendering.

We prepared a peaceful demonstration, with Razoua commanding our battalions from Montmartre. Because our friends who were armed were determined for the demonstration to be peaceful, they withdrew with their weapons, even though peaceful demonstrations are always crushed.

When only a disarmed multitude remained, soldiers in the buildings around the square opened fire on us. No shot was fired by the people before the Breton Mobiles fired their volleys. We could see the pale faces of the Bretons behind the windows, as a noise like hail sounded in our ears. Yes, you fired on us, you untamed Celts, but at least it was your faith that made you fanatics for the counter-revolution. You weren't bought by the reactionaries. You killed us, but you believed you were doing your duty, and some day we will convert you to our ideals of liberty.

On February 22, the Committees of Vigilance were closed down, and newspaper publication was suspended. The Versailles reactionaries decided they had to disarm Paris. Napoleon III was still alive, and with Montmartre disarmed, the entrance of a monarch, either Bonaparte or an Orleanist, would have favored the army, which was either an accomplice of the reactionaries or was allowing itself to be deceived. With Montmartre disarmed, the Prussian Army, which was sitting in the surrendered forts around Paris while the armistice continued, would have been protected.

The declaration of the Commune in March 1871 led to ongoing military conflict. For three months, the people of Paris resisted the forces of General Thiers.

During the entire time of the Commune, I only spent one night at my poor mother's. I never really went to bed during that time; I just napped a little whenever there was nothing better to do, and many other people lived the same way. Everybody who wanted deliverance gave himself totally to the cause.

During the Commune I went unhurt except for a bullet that grazed my wrist, although my hat was literally riddled with bullet holes. I did twist my ankle, which had been sprained for a long time, and because I couldn't walk for three or four days, I had to requisition a carriage…

While I was going to Montmartre for the funeral, I hadn't dared to stop off at my mother's, because she would have seen that I had a sprain. Several days before the funeral, though, I had come face to face with her in the trenches near the railroad station of Clamart. She had come to see if all the lies I had written to soothe her were true. Fortunately, she always ended up believing me.

If the reaction had had as many enemies among women as it did among men, the Versailles Government would have had a more difficult task subduing us. Our male friends are more susceptible to faintheartedness than we women are. A supposedly weak woman knows better than any man how to say: "It must be done." She may feel ripped open to her very womb, but she remains unmoved. Without hate, without anger, without pity for herself or others, whether her heart bleeds or not, she can say: "It must be done." Such were the women of the Commune. During Bloody Week, women erected and defended the barricade at the Place Blanche — and held it till they died.

In my mind I feel the soft darkness of a spring night. It is May 1871, and I see the red reflection of flames. It is Paris afire. That fire is a dawn, and I see it still as I sit here writing. Memory crowds in on me, and I keep forgetting that I am writing my memoirs.

In the night of May 22 or 23, I believe, we were at the Montmartre cemetery, which we were trying to defend with too few fighters. We had crenelated the walls as best we could, and, the position wasn't bad except for the battery on the Butte of Montmartre — now in the hands of the reactionaries, and whose fire raked us — the shells were coming at regular intervals from the side, where tall houses commanded our defenses. Shells tore the air, marking time like a clock...

In spite of my comrades' advice, I chose to walk there several times. Always the shells arrived too early or too late for me. One shell falling across the trees covered me with flowered branches, which I divided up between two tombs.

My comrades caught me, and one ordered me not to move about. They made me sit down on a bench. But nothing is as stubborn as a woman. In the midst of all this, Jaroslav Dombrowski passed in front of us sadly, on his way to be killed. "It's over," he told me. "No, no," I said to him, and he held out both his hands to me. But he was right.

Three hundred thousand voices had elected the Commune. Fifteen thousand stood up to the clash with the army during Bloody Week.

We've counted about 35,000 people who were executed, but how many were there that we know nothing of? From time to time the earth disgorges its corpses. If we are implacable in the coming fight, who is to blame?

The Commune, surrounded from every direction, had only death on its horizon. It could only be brave, and it was. And in dying it opened wide the door to the future. That was its destiny.

From: Louise Michel, *Mémoires* (Trans. —*Ed.*)

Louise Michel
Letter to the Mayor of Montmartre, Georges Clemenceau

Sir,

Our Women's Republican Vigilance Committee in the 18th arron-dissement is wanting to play its part in our patriotic task.

Given the people's poverty, and no longer able to bear the sight of babes-in-arms who are dying of hunger, I ask you to take the following initiatives:

- Launch an immediate inquiry in each house in the 18th arrondissement, in order to determine the number of old people, infirm and children.
- Immediately requisition all abandoned housing in the 18th arrondissement, in order to house all homeless citizens and establish shelters where children can be fed.
- That all wine and coal in the cellars of abandoned houses immediately be made available for the use of the infirm and sick.
- The complete abolition within the 18th arrondissement of all brothels and workhouses for young girls.
- Melt down the Bells of Montmartre to make cannon.

The acting president,
Louise Michel
24 rue Oudot, Montmartre

Louise Michel
Letter to the Editors of *La Sociale* newspaper

The women volunteering as ambulance drivers for the Paris Commune would like to take a moment to salute you.

They hope that you would publish the following declaration because, at this moment, the person who does not affirm their position, like one who flees from conflict, is a coward:

The ambulance workers of the Commune declare that they do not belong to any association whatever. They live their lives entirely for the revolution. Their duty, even on the very field of battle, is to dress the wounds made by the poisoned bullets from Versailles, or as the hour requires, to take up a rifle like all the others.

In the case that the reaction triumphs — and we hope that this will never happen — their duty, which they will never forget, is to set fire to the gunpowder. Wherever this happens, the revolution must never be defeated.

Long live the Commune!
Long live the universal republic!

The volunteer ambulance workers of the Commune,
Louise Michel, Fernandez, Goullé, Poulain, Quartier Dauguet.

Xavière Gauthier (ed.), *Louise Michel, je vous écris de ma nuit*. (Trans. —*Ed.*)

chapter four: *When the Women Decide They Have Had Enough*

Throughout the Commune, women organized themselves in local community associations. Louise Michel played a leading role in mobilizing women in support of the Commune. But in her Memoirs, *Michel downplayed her own leadership role as chair of the Women's Vigilance Committee during the Commune's period of rule.*

On April 11, 1871, just weeks after the seizure of power by the Commune, a group of women issued "A call to the women citizens of Paris." The pamphlet called for the creation of women's associations around Paris, and led to the formation of the Union des Femmes pour la Défense de Paris et les Soins aux Blessés (Association of Women for the Defense of Paris and Aid to the Wounded). Key leaders included Nathalie Lemel (later exiled to New Caledonia with Louise Michel), and a young Russian activist, Elisabeth Dmitrieff, who was a member of Karl Marx's First International. Dmitrieff was influential in bringing women's demands to the Commune, seeking resources so that women could organize for themselves.

Women activists like Dmitrieff moved beyond basic demands to put forward socialist proposals to the leaders of the Paris Commune. They called for the implementation of the decree on abandoned workshops, issued by the Commune on April 16, so that women could find work in factories abandoned by bourgeois owners fleeing the revolution.

In her classic study Women, Resistance and Revolution, *English feminist Sheila Rowbotham argues that their experience in the Commune pushed Parisian women toward a feminist view of the world.*

Louise Michel
On women's rights

In 1870, the first organization of the Rights of Women had begun to meet on the Rue Thevenot. At the meetings of the Rights of Women group, and at other meetings, the most advanced men applauded the idea of equality. I noticed — I had seen it before, and I saw it later — that men, their declarations notwithstanding, although they appeared to help us, were always content with just the appearance. This was the result of custom and the force of old prejudices, and it convinced me that we women must simply take our place without begging for it...

The issue of political rights is dead. Equal education, equal trades, so that prostitution would not be the only lucrative profession open to a woman — that is what was real in our program. The Russian revolutionaries are right: evolution is ended and now revolution is necessary or the butterfly will die in its cocoon.

Heroic women were found in all social classes. At the professional school, women of all social levels met together, and all would have preferred to die rather than surrender. They organized the Society for the Victims of the War. They dispensed their resources the best way they could, while demanding that Paris resist, and continue to resist, the Prussian siege...

Later, when I was a prisoner, the first visitor I had was Madame Meurice from the Society for the Victims of the War. At my last trial, behind the handpicked spectators, I spotted the shining eyes of two other former members of the society among those who had managed to squeeze in.

I salute all those brave women of the vanguard who were drawn from group to group: the Women's Vigilance Committee, the women's associations, and later the League of Women. The old world ought to fear the day when those women finally decide they have had enough. Those women will not slack off. Strength finds refuge in them. Beware of them!

Beware of those who go across Europe waving the flag of liberty, and beware of the most peaceful daughter of Gaul now asleep in the deep resignation of the fields. Beware of the women when they are sickened by all that is around them and rise up against the old world. On that day the new world will begin.

From: *The Red Virgin — Memoirs of Louise Michel.*
Extracts from Part One, X–XIV.

Parisian Women

A call to the women citizens of Paris (April 11, 1871)

…The fratricidal madness that has taken possession of France, this duel unto death, is the final act in the eternal antagonism between right and might, labor and exploitation, the people and their tyrants!

The privileged classes of the present social order are our enemies; those who have lived by our labor, thriving on our want.

They have seen the people rise up, demanding: "No obligations without rights! No rights without obligations! We want to work but we also want the product of our work. No more exploiters. No more bosses. Work and security for all — The people to govern themselves — We want the Commune; we want to live in freedom or to die fighting for it!"…

Women of Paris, the decisive hour has come. The old world must come to an end! We want to be free! And France has not risen up alone. The civilized nations of the world have their eyes on Paris. They are waiting for our victory to free themselves in their turn…

[signed]
A group of Parisian women

NOTICE:
We invite patriotic women citizens to meet today, Tuesday, April 11… in order to take concrete measures toward the formation of committees, in each arrondissement, aimed at organizing a women's movement for the defense of Paris, in the event that reaction and its gendarmes should attempt to capture it.

We require the active collaboration of all the women of Paris who realize that the salvation of our capital depends on the outcome of this conflict; who know that the present social order bears in itself the seeds of poverty and the death of freedom and of justice; who therefore welcome the advent of the reign of labor and of equality and are prepared at the hour of peril to fight and to die for the triumph of this revolution, for which our brothers are sacrificing their lives!

From: *Journal Officiel* (Commune). April 11, 1871.

Women Citizens of Paris
Request for organizational assistance from the Commune

To: Executive Commission of the Paris Commune
April 14, 1871

Considering:

That it is the duty and the right of everyone to fight for the sacred cause of the people, that is, for the revolution;

That danger is imminent and that the enemy are at the gates of Paris;

That union makes strength; in time of danger all individual efforts must combine to form a collective, invincible resistance by the whole population;

That the Commune — representing the principle of extinction of all privilege and all inequality — should therefore consider all legitimate grievances of any section of the population without discrimination of sex, such discrimination having been made and enforced as a means of maintaining the privileges of the ruling classes;

That the success of the present conflict, whose aim is to put an end to corruption, and ultimately to regenerate society by ensuring the rule of labor and justice, is of as much significance to the women as it is to the men of Paris;

That many among them are resolved that in the event of the enemy breaking into Paris, they will fight to the finish in defense of our common rights;

That effective organization of this revolutionary element into a vigorous defensive force for the Paris Commune can only be achieved with concrete aid from the government of the Commune itself;

Consequently, the delegates of the women citizens of Paris request the Executive Commission of the Commune:

1. To order all district town halls to make available in each district a room that can serve as headquarters of the committees;

2. To request that they provide large premises for meetings of women citizens;

3. To have the Commune subsidize the printing of circulars, posters and notices that these committees decide to distribute.

For the members of the Central Committee of Women Citizens,
[Signed by seven women workers and E. Dmitrieff]

From: *Journal Officiel* (Commune). April 14, 1871.

Elisabeth Dmitrieff

Letter from the Association of Women to the Commune's Commission of Labor and Exchange

The Association of Women have considered the following:

There is only one way of reorganizing labor so that the producer is guaranteed the product of his own work, and that is by setting up free producer associations which will share out the profits from the various industries.

The setting up of these associations would put an end to the exploitation and enslavement of labor by capital, and would at last guarantee the workers the management of their own affairs. It would simultaneously facilitate urgently needed reforms, in both production and producer relationships, to include the following points:

1) Variety of work in each trade — continually repeated manual movement damages both mind and body.

2) A reduction in working hours — physical exhaustion inevitably destroys man's spiritual qualities.

3) An end to all competition between male and female workers — their interests are identical and their solidarity is essential to the success of the final worldwide strike of labor against capital.

The association therefore wants:

1) Equal pay for equal hours of work.

2) A local and international federation of the various trade sections in order to ease the movement and exchange of goods by centralizing the international interests of the producers.

The general development of these producer associations requires:

1) Informing and organizing the working masses... The conse-

quence of this will be that every association member will be expected to belong to the International Working Men's Association.

2) State assistance in advancing the necessary credit for setting up these associations: loans repayable in yearly instalments at a rate of five percent.

The reorganization of female labor is an extremely urgent matter, when one considers that in the society of the past it was the most exploited form of all.

Faced by the present events, with poverty increasing at an alarming rate, and seeing the unwarranted halt in all work, it is to be feared that the women of Paris, who have become momentarily revolutionary in spirit, may as a result of the state of continual privation, relapse into the more or less reactionary and passive position which the social order of the past marked out for them. That would be a disastrous step backwards which would endanger the revolutionary and international interests of the working class, thereby endangering the Commune.

For these reasons the Central Committee of the Association of Women requests the Commune's Commission on Labor and Exchange to entrust it with the reorganization and allocation of work for the women of Paris, in the first instance providing the association with production of military supplies.

This work will naturally not be sufficient for the majority of working women, so in addition the Central Committee requests the commission to place at the disposal of the federated producer associations the sums of money necessary for the working of the factories and workshops abandoned by the bourgeois and comprising those crafts mainly practised by women, like:

> Brush-making
> Bandage-making
> Haberdashery
> *Passementerie* (trimmings)
> Flower and plume work

Embroidery
Assembly of umbrellas, straw hats, banners and flags
Cap-making
Illuminating
Fan-making
Typographing
Typesetting
Coloring
Making of pasteboard articles
Glass blowing (pearls)
Button-making
Millinery
Lingerie (underclothing)
Book-stitching
Bookbinding
Laundering
Kennel-work
Porcelain-painting
Corset-making
Wreath-making
Waistcoat-making
Doll-dressing
Tie-making

For the Executive Commission,
The Secretary General E. Dmitrieff.

chapter five: *The First Dress Rehearsal in World History*

The Paris Commune, which only lasted between March and May 1871, has taken on legendary importance for a range of anarchists, socialists and communists. Karl Marx published his famous pamphlet The Civil War in France *just days after the Commune was crushed, and the revolt of the Paris workers was later analyzed by theorists from different political traditions.*

Here are some excerpts about the Commune by Karl Marx and Friedrich Engels, authors of The Communist Manifesto; *anarchist leaders Peter Kropotkin and Mikhail Bakunin; English artist and socialist William Morris; V.I. Lenin, leader of the Russian Bolshevik Party; and contemporary socialists and historians like Howard Zinn, Paul Foot and Sheila Rowbotham.*

All these writers and political activists celebrate the Commune as the first major example of a workers' government — but they draw different lessons about the role of political organization, how workers can organize themselves, and whether to abolish the institutions of the state.

Karl Marx

The working class did not expect miracles from the Commune. They have no ready-made utopias to introduce. They know that in order to work out their own emancipation, and along with it that higher form to which present society is irresistibly tending by its own economical agencies, they will have to pass through long struggles, through a series of historic processes, transforming circumstances and men. They have no ideals to realize, but to set free the elements of the new society with which the old collapsing bourgeois society itself is pregnant...

When the Paris Commune took the management of the revolution in its own hands; when plain working men for the first time dared to infringe upon the governmental privilege of their "natural superiors" and, under circumstances of unexampled difficulty, performed their work modestly, conscientiously and efficiently... the old world writhed in convulsions of rage at the sight of the red flag, the symbol of the republic of labor, floating over the Hôtel de Ville.

And yet, this was the first revolution in which the working class was openly acknowledged as the only class capable of social initiative, even by the great bulk of the Paris middle class — shopkeepers, tradesmen, merchants — the wealthy capitalists alone excepted.

From: Karl Marx, *The Civil War in France.*

Friedrich Engels

From the very outset the Commune was compelled to recognize that the working class, once come to power, could not go on managing with the old state machine; that in order not to lose again its only just-conquered supremacy, this working class must, on the one hand, do away with all the old repressive machinery previously used against it, and, on the other, safeguard itself against its own deputies and officials, by declaring them all, without exception, subject to recall at any moment.

What had been the characteristic attribute of the former state? Society had created its own organs to look after its common interests, originally through simple division of labor. But these organs, at whose head was the state power, had in the course of time, in pursuance of their own special interests, transformed themselves from the servants of society into the masters of society.

This can be seen, for example, not only in the hereditary monarchy, but equally so in the democratic republic. Nowhere do "politicians" form a more separate and powerful section of the nation than precisely in North America. There, each of the two major parties which alternately succeed each other in power is itself in turn controlled by people who make a business of politics, who speculate on seats in the legislative assemblies of the union as well as of the separate states, or who make a living by carrying on agitation for their party and on its victory are rewarded with positions. It is well known how the Americans have been trying for 30 years to shake off this yoke, which has become intolerable, and how in spite of it all they continue to sink ever deeper in this swamp of corruption.

It is precisely in North America that we see best how there takes place this process of the state power making itself independent in relation to society, whose mere instrument it was originally intended to be. Here there exists no dynasty, no nobility, no standing army, beyond the few men keeping watch on the Indians, no bureaucracy with permanent posts or the right to pensions. And nevertheless we find here two great gangs of political speculators, who alternately take possession of the state power and exploit it by the most corrupt means and for the most corrupt ends — and the nation is powerless against these two great cartels of politicians, who are ostensibly its servants, but in reality dominate and plunder it.

From: Friedrich Engels, "Introduction" to *The Civil War in France*.

Mikhail Bakunin

I am a supporter of the Paris Commune, which for all the blood-
letting it suffered at the hands of the monarchical and clerical reaction, has nonetheless grown more enduring and more powerful in
the hearts and minds of the European proletariat. I am its supporter,
above all, because it was a bold, clearly formulated negation of the
state. It is immensely significant that this rebellion against the state
has taken place in France, which had been hitherto the land of
political centralization par excellence, and that it was precisely
Paris, the leader and the fountainhead of the great French civilization, which took the initiative in the Commune.

The small group of convinced socialists who participated in the
Commune were in a very difficult position. While they felt the lack of
support from the great masses of the people of Paris, and while the
organization of the International Working Men's Association, itself
imperfect, comprised hardly a few thousand persons, they had to
keep up a daily struggle against the Jacobin majority. In the midst
of the conflict, they had to feed and provide work for several thous-
and workers, organize and arm them, and keep a sharp lookout for
the doings of the reactionaries. All this in an immense city like Paris,
besieged, facing the threat of starvation, and prey to all the shady
intrigues of the reaction, which managed to establish itself in Versailles with the permission and by the grace of the Prussians. They
had to set up a revolutionary government and army against the government and army of Versailles; in order to fight the monarchist and
clerical reaction they were compelled to organize themselves in a
Jacobin manner, forgetting or sacrificing the first conditions of
revolutionary socialism...

Contrary to the belief of authoritarian communists — which I
deem completely wrong — that a social revolution must be decreed

and organized either by a dictatorship or by a constituent assembly emerging from a political revolution, our friends, the Paris socialists, believed that revolution could neither be made nor brought to its full development except by the spontaneous and continued action of the masses, the groups and the associations of the people. Our Paris friends were right a thousand times over... the social revolution should end by granting full liberty to the masses, the groups, the communes, the associations and to the individuals as well; by destroying once and for all the historic cause of all violence, which is the power and indeed the mere existence of the state. Its fall will bring down with it all the inequities of the law and all the lies of the various religions, since both law and religion have never been anything but the compulsory consecration, ideal and real, of all violence represented, guaranteed and protected by the state.

From: Mikhail Aleksandrovich Bakunin,
The Paris Commune and the Idea of the State
(New York: Alfred A. Knopf, 1871).

William Morris

It should be noted that the risings which took place in other towns in France were not so much vanquished by the strength of the bourgeoisie, which at first found itself powerless before the people, but rather fell through owing to a want of fuller development of socialism and a more vigorous proclamation of its principles.

The whole revolt was at last drowned in the blood of the workers of Paris. Certainly the immediate result was to crush socialism for the time by the destruction of a whole generation of its most determined recruits. Nevertheless the very violence and excess of the bourgeois revenge have, as we can now see, tended to strengthen the progress of socialism, as they have set the seal of tragedy and heroism on the mixed events of the Commune, and made its memory a rallying point for all future revolutionists.

From: William Morris, "The Paris Commune of 1871, and the Continental Movement Following It," *Socialism From The Roots Up* (in *Commonweal*, Volume 2, No. 38, October 2, 1886) 210.

Peter Kropotkin

The Commune of 1871 could be nothing but a first attempt. Beginning at the close of a war, hemmed in between two armies ready to join hands and crush the people, it dared not unhesitatingly set forth upon the path of economic revolution; it neither boldly declared itself socialist, nor proceeded with the expropriation of capital or the organization of labor. It did not even take stock of the general resources of the city. Nor did it break with the tradition of the state, of representative government. It did not seek to establish within the Commune that organization from the simple to the complex which it inaugurated by proclaiming the independence and free federation of the communes. Yet it is certain that if the Paris Commune had lived a few months longer it would inevitably have been driven by the force of circumstances toward both these revolutions.

Let us not forget that the bourgeoisie took four years of a revolutionary period to change a limited monarchy into a bourgeois republic, and we should not be astonished that the people of Paris did not cross with a single bound the space between the anarchist Commune and the government of robbers. But let us also bear in mind that the next revolution, which in France and certainly in Spain as well will be communalist, will take up the work of the Paris Commune where it was checked by the massacres of the Versailles Army.

The Commune was defeated, and too well we know how the middle class avenged itself for the scare given it by the people when they shook their rulers' yoke loose upon their necks. It proved that there really are two classes in our modern society; on one side, the man who works and yields up to the monopolists of property more than half of what he produces and yet lightly passes over the wrong done him by his masters; on the other, the idler, the spoiler, hating his slave, ready to kill him like game, animated by the most savage instincts as soon as he is menaced in his possession.

From: Peter Kropotkin, "The Commune of Paris,"
Freedom Pamphlets No. 2 (London: W. Reeves, 1895).
Based on the original French version published in
Le Révolté, March 20, 1880.

V.I. Lenin

Forty years have passed since the proclamation of the Paris Commune. In accordance with tradition, the French workers paid homage to the memory of the men and women of the revolution of March 18, 1871, by meetings and demonstrations. At the end of May they will again place wreaths on the graves of the Communards who were shot, the victims of the terrible "May Week," and over their graves they will once more vow to fight untiringly until their ideas have triumphed and the cause they bequeathed has been fully achieved...

[I]n spite of its brief existence, the Commune managed to promulgate a few measures which sufficiently characterize its real significance and aims. The Commune did away with the standing army, that blind weapon in the hands of the ruling classes, and armed the whole people. It proclaimed the separation of church and state, abolished state payments to religious bodies (i.e., state salaries for priests), made popular education purely secular, and in this way struck a severe blow at the gendarmes in cassocks. In the purely social sphere the Commune accomplished very little, but this little nevertheless clearly reveals its character as a popular, workers' government. Night work in bakeries was forbidden; the system of fines, which represented legalized robbery of the workers, was abolished. Finally, there was the famous decree that all factories and workshops abandoned or shut down by their owners were to be turned over to associations of workers that were to resume production. And, as if to emphasize its character as a truly democratic, proletarian government, the Commune decreed that the salaries of all administrative and government officials, irrespective of rank, should not exceed the normal wages of a worker, and in no case amount to more than 6,000 francs a year (less than 200 rubles a month).

All these measures showed clearly enough that the Commune

was a deadly menace to the old world founded on the enslavement and exploitation of the people. That was why bourgeois society could not feel at ease so long as the Red Flag of the proletariat waved over the Hôtel de Ville in Paris. And when the organized forces of the government finally succeeded in gaining the upper hand over the poorly organized forces of the revolution, the Bonapartist generals... organized such a slaughter as Paris had never known. About 30,000 Parisians were shot down by the bestial soldiery, and about 45,000 were arrested, many of whom were afterwards executed, while thousands were transported or exiled. In all, Paris lost about 100,000 of its best people, including some of the finest workers in all trades...

The memory of the fighters of the Commune is honored not only by the workers of France but by the proletariat of the whole world. For the Commune fought, not for some local or narrow national aim, but for the emancipation of all toiling humanity, of all the downtrodden and oppressed. As a foremost fighter for the social revolution, the Commune has won sympathy wherever there is a proletariat suffering and engaged in struggle. The epic of its life and death, the sight of a workers' government which seized the capital of the world and held it for over two months, the spectacle of the heroic struggle of the proletariat and the torments it underwent after its defeat — all this raised the spirit of millions of workers, aroused their hopes and enlisted their sympathy for the cause of socialism. The thunder of the cannon in Paris awakened the most backward sections of the proletariat from their deep slumber, and everywhere gave impetus to the growth of revolutionary socialist propaganda. That is why the cause of the Commune is not dead. It lives to the present day in every one of us...

From: V.I. Lenin & Karl Marx, *The Civil War in France: The Paris Commune*, (New York: International Publishers, 1940).

Howard Zinn

There is still a widespread popular belief, heavily stressed on the *Readers' Digest* level, that Marxism believes in the supremacy of the state over the individual, while democracy believes the opposite. In fact, the existence of oppressively overbearing states in the world, which call themselves Marxist, reinforces this idea. But a true radicalism would remind people in both socialist and capitalist countries of Marx's and Engels' hope, expressed early in the *[Communist] Manifesto,* that some day "the public power will lose its political character" and "we shall have an association in which the free development of each is the condition for the free development of all." This is not just a youthful aberration (there is a fad about the young romantic Marx and the old, practical Marx) because 27 years later, Marx, in his *Critique of the Gotha Program,* says: "Freedom consists in converting the state from an organ superimposed upon society into one completely subordinate to it." Here also he says, on the subject of the state giving education to the people, "the state has need, on the contrary, of a very stern education by the people." And Engels, a year after Marx's death, in 1884, writes in his *Origin of the Family, Private Property and the State*:

> The society that will organize production on the basis of a free and equal association of the producers will put the whole machinery of state where it will then belong: into the museum of antiquities, by the side of the spinning wheel and the bronze axe.

Their attitude to the state is made even clearer and more specific in Marx's book on *The Civil War in France,* and Engels' "Introduction" to it; where both of them point admiringly to the Paris Commune of early 1871. The Commune almost immediately abolished conscription and the standing army; declared universal suffrage and the right of citizens to recall their elected officials at any time; said all officials, high or low, should be paid the same wage as received by other workers, and publicly burned the guillotine.

The New Left is anti-authoritarian; it would, I expect, burn draft cards in any society. It is anarchistic not just in wanting the ultimate abolition of the state, but in its immediate requirement that authority and coercion be banished in every sphere of existence, that the end must be represented immediately in the means. Marx and Bakunin disagreed on this, but the New Left has the advantage over Marx of having an extra century of history to study. We see how a dictatorship of the proletariat can easily become a dictatorship over the proletariat, as Trotsky warned, as Rosa Luxemburg warned. The New Left should remind the socialist states as well as the capitalist states of Marx's letter of 1853 to the *New York Tribune* saying he didn't know how capital punishment could be justified "in a society glorying in its civilization."

From: Howard Zinn, "The New Radicalism,"
The Howard Zinn Reader —
Writings on Disobedience and Democracy
(New York: Seven Stories, 1997).

Paul Foot

Millions of words have been written about the Commune but the most exhilarating and accurate account is still that of Karl Marx. His *Civil War in France*, which he wrote as the Commune was being defeated, and which includes a glorious passage of sustained invective against Thiers, is one of the clearest and most passionate political pamphlets ever written. It is impossible to read it 130 years later without being inspired by the vision and application of the Communards, whose simple aspirations contrast so grotesquely with the complacent and corrupt behavior of modern politicians on both sides of the [English] Channel.

The objection to parliamentary democracy is not that it is democratic or representative, but that it is nothing like democratic or representative enough. The revolutionary writer and fighter Karl Marx wrote 130 years ago about the revolutionary Paris Commune in 1871. He noted three central features. First, it was freely elected by a majority. Second, its representatives got the same wages as the people who elected them. And third, the elected government formed the executive as well as the legislative power. That means that it not only passed the laws, usually in the form of decrees, but also carried them out. The forms of the new power made it possible to convert political promises into political action.

Similar alternatives to ordinary parliamentary institutions have occurred again and again through the 20th century — in Russia in 1905 and 1917, in Germany and Hungary in 1919 and the ensuing years, in Spain in 1936, in Hungary in 1956, and in Portugal in 1974. In the best cases workers threw up organizations based on elected councils, with their representatives paid the same and subject to instant recall. These councils were more efficient and effective representatives than their parliamentary equivalents because they were more democratic. They formed themselves quite naturally in the struggle for emancipation by the exploited masses. And they all emerged at times of revolution. The reason for that is very simple. The existing power structure, including parliamentary democracy, is tolerated by the controllers of wealth only as long as that control is not threatened.

It follows that the only real democratic alternatives to parliamentary democracy can emerge when the minority control of the capitalists is challenged. In each of these cases of revolution, the pendulum swung back to different points of reaction — either to terrible tyrannies or to parliamentary democracies every bit as feeble as before.

The chief reason for this decline was the failure of the revolutionary forces to organize their new strength, to unite their forces powerfully enough to stave off the reaction and move forward to a new social order. It is a grim irony of history that on the one occasion where the revolutionaries were led by a party — Russia in October 1917 — the working-class base of that party was destroyed in civil war before it could consolidate its advances.

The lessons are plain. There are democratic alternatives to parliament, but they are only likely to emerge when there is a challenge from below to the economic rule of the minority.

How can we encourage such a challenge? Revolutions cannot be created out of thin air. They can only arise in an atmosphere of confidence. So the only way to work for a revolution and a more democratic society is to relate to the day-to-day struggles that always absorb the exploited lives of the working people. Every strike, every demonstration, every manifestation of revolt carries with it the seed of revolution. The pompous and self-absorbed activities of the representatives of parliamentary democracy work against such a revolution because they constantly dampen down, mock and humiliate live protest. They pretend they are democrats, but by their actions prove the opposite. The seeds of a new, more democratic society can only be sown in struggle against the old one.

From: Paul Foot: "Last time Paris went left,"
The Guardian, London. March 20, 2001.

Sheila Rowbotham

The idea of a march of women to Versailles to stop the bloodshed spread in April 1871. Beatrice Excoffon, the daughter of a watchmaker who lived with a compositor, told her mother she was leaving, kissed her children, and joined the procession at the Place de la Concorde. There were about 700 to 800 women. Nobody was clear about the aims of the march or knew definitely what they should do, but there were political rather than strictly economic motives.

Some talked about explaining to Versailles what Paris wanted. Others talked about how things were a hundred years ago when the women of Paris had gone to Versailles to carry off the baker and the baker's little boy, as they said then.

Also the role of women had been raised. There was a dispute about whether women could only ask for peace or whether they should defend their country as much as the men. For although the women had been taking action, they had been taking action from their traditional position as women. Rather similar was the way in which they walked ahead of their men in the Commune to meet the soldiers, saying "Will you fire on us? On your brothers, our husbands? Our children?"

These actions were still from a quite customary definition of womanliness. Although revolutionary political ideas were impinging on these women and although they acted with conscious historical memory, they were not challenging in any way their role as women. However, very easily in such moments the new conception of commitment could upset what had been regarded as the woman's sphere. A head-on clash could ensue between what the women felt to be their duty and what the men felt it to be, as wives, daughters, mothers. Thus in 1792 when the women's battalions were formed in the French Revolution there was opposition from the men. In challenging the men's sole right to patriotism and glory the revolutionary women moved into a form of feminism. There was a similar development in 1871. One source of feminist consciousness here came from the attempt to equalize revolutionary struggle. A women's battalion was not allowed but the women of the Commune accompanied their husbands or lovers and often fought with them. *La Sociale* reported on April 5: "A band of women armed with chassepots today passed by the Place de la Concorde. They were going to join the Commune fighters."

Often the dividing lines between nursing at one of the first aid posts, serving as a *cantinière* or being a soldier were not clear. On the battlefield Louise Michel, a schoolteacher prominent in the Commune, looked after the wounded and took part in the fighting. The accounts these women leave describe their complete commitment to the Commune. They lived only for the revolution in a way which is only possible in times of extreme crisis. But they were not always well regarded by the officers. Andre Leo, a revolutionary feminist who was a journalist, described how obstacles were put in their way by the officers and surgeons who were hostile even though the troops were in favor of them. She believed that this division was because the officers still retained the narrow consciousness of military men while the soldiers were equally revolutionary citizens. She felt this prejudice had had serious political consequences.

In the first revolution women had been excluded from freedom and equality; they had returned to Catholicism and reaction. Andre Leo maintained that the republicans were inconsistent. They did not want women to be under the sway of the priests, but they were upset when women were freethinkers and wanted to act like free human beings. Republican men were just replacing the authority of emperor and God with their own. They still needed subjects, or at least subjected women. They did not want to admit anymore than the revolutionaries of the 1790s that woman was responsible to herself.

"She should remain neutral and passive, under the guidance of man. She will have done nothing to change her confessor."

Yet this was the very antithesis of all the claims of revolutionary ideas. It was evident that, "The revolution is the liberty and responsibility of every human being, limited only by the rights of all, without privilege of race or sex." Thus by taking the revolution seriously the women of the Commune also found themselves forced to take up feminist positions in that they had to struggle not only against the enemy at Versailles but to confront the prejudice and suspicion of some of the men on their own side. The experience was one which was subsequently to be repeated in other revolutionary movements.

It is at the point when the revolution starts to move women out of their passivity into the conscious and active role of militants that the mockery, the caricatures, the laughter with strong sexual undertones begin. It is one of the most effective weapons against women's emergence. It is one thing to be the object of hatred and insults, and another to be the object of scorn and hilarity as well. It produces its own self-mocking defenses and its own peculiar paralysis.

If there was some ambiguity in the attitude of the men of the left there was none in that of the men of the right. Here class hatred, political elitism and sexual authoritarianism united in hysterical denunciation and acts of atrocity. Listen to Maxime du Camp on the women:

"Those who gave themselves to the Commune — and there were many — had but a single ambition: to raise themselves above the level of man by exaggerating his vices. There they found an ideal they could achieve. They were venomous and cowardly. They were all there agitating and squawking: inmates from Saint-Lazare out on the spree... the vendors of modes *à la tripe de Caen;* the gentlemen's seamstresses; the gentlemen's shirtmakers; the teachers of grown-up schoolboys... What was profoundly comic was that these absconders from the workhouse unfailingly invoked Joan of Arc, and were not above comparing themselves to her... During the final days, all of these bellicose viragos held out longer than the men did behind the barricades. Many of them were arrested, with powder-blackened hands and shoulders bruised by the recoil of their rifles; they were still palpitating from the overstimulation of battle."

The penalties were severe. Beside the names which are well known, like Louise Michel, sentenced to transportation to a penal settlement, there were innumerable others. A concierge, Louise Noel; a parasol-maker, Jeanne Laymet; a cook, Eugenie Lhilly; the seamstress, Eulalie Papavoine; Elizabeth Retiffe, a cardboard-maker; the rag-picker Marie Wolff — they were transported, given hard labor and executed. They had gone to join their lovers on the barricades or they had been moved by the sight of the wounded. They loved the republic, hated the rich, and rose against the years of humiliation they had experienced as workers and as women.

Captain Jouenne began the indictment at their trial by calling them, "unworthy creatures who seem to have taken it on themselves to become an opprobrium to their sex, and to repudiate the great and magnificent role of woman in society... a legitimate wife, the object of our affection and respect, entirely devoted to her family... But if, deserting this sacred mission, the nature of her influence changes, and serves none but the spirit of evil, she becomes a moral monstrosity; then woman is more dangerous than the most dangerous man."

There was a change too in the way she was treated by the gentlemen of the ruling class. Elisée Reclus, the geographer taken prisoner, described one of the women canteen workers:

"The poor woman was in the row in front of mine, at the side of her husband. She was not at all pretty, nor was she young: rather a poor, middle-aged proletarian, small, marching with difficulty. Insults rained down on her, all from officers prancing on horseback along the road. A very young officer said, 'You know what we're going to do with her? We're going to screw her with a red hot iron.' A vast horrified silence fell among the soldiers."

Here expressed in a particularly intense and repulsive form was the hypocrisy which the young Marx had exposed so vehemently. Here is the real nature of the sensibility and gallantry of the men of the upper classes toward femininity.

From: Sheila Rowbotham,
Women, Resistance and Revolution
(London: Penguin, 1972).

chapter six: *"The Internationale"*

The events of the Paris Commune inspired the famous revolutionary hymn — "The Internationale." Eugène Pottier wrote the original French lyrics in June 1871 while in jail after the defeat of the Commune. Pottier, a fabric designer, had participated in the 1848 revolt in France and was elected to the Paris Commune in March 1871. He was a close friend of the French painter Gustave Courbet, an admirer of Pierre-Joseph Proudhon (the campaigner for anti-authoritarian socialism) and a member of the First International. Following the Commune, Pottier fled to England and the United States and was condemned to death in his absence by the French authorities.

Pottier's poem was set to music by Pierre Degeyter in 1888, one year after his death. The song rapidly became a favorite of the European workers' movement and the hymn of socialists and communists, to be sung at conferences of the First and Second Internationals. It was adopted as the first National Anthem of the Soviet Union, then the anthem of the (third) Communist International, until Stalin changed it during World War II. However, as sung by the Chinese students and workers at Tienanmen Square in Beijing, it remains a song of protest and revolt.

"The Internationale"
Words by Eugène Pottier (Paris 1871)
Music by Pierre Degeyter (1888)

Arise ye workers from your slumbers
Arise ye prisoners of want
For reason in revolt now thunders
And at last ends the age of cant.
Away with all your superstitions
Servile masses arise, arise
We'll change henceforth the old tradition
And spurn the dust to win the prize.

Chorus:
So comrades, come rally
And the last fight let us face
"The Internationale" unites the human race.
So comrades, come rally
And the last fight let us face
"The Internationale" unites the human race.

No more deluded by reaction
On tyrants only we'll make war
The soldiers too will take strike action
They'll break ranks and fight no more
And if those cannibals keep trying
To sacrifice us to their pride
They soon shall hear the bullets flying
We'll shoot the generals on our own side.

No savior from on high delivers
No faith have we in prince or peer
Our own right hand the chains must shiver
Chains of hatred, greed and fear
E'er the thieves will out with their booty
And give to all a happier lot.
Each at the forge must do their duty
And we'll strike while the iron is hot.

V.I. Lenin
The workers' anthem

In 1913, on the 25th anniversary of Pottier's death, the Russian revolutionary Vladimir Lenin stated:

This song has been translated into all European and other languages. In whatever country a class-conscious worker finds himself, wherever fate may cast him, however much he may feel himself a stranger, without language, without friends, far from his native country — he can find himself comrades and friends by the familiar refrain of "The Internationale."

The workers of all countries have adopted the song of their foremost fighter, the proletarian poet, and have made it the worldwide song of the proletariat.

From: V.I. Lenin, *Collected Works, Volume 36* (Moscow: Progress Publishers, 1966), 223–224. Originally published in *Pravda,* January 3, 1913.

chapter seven: *Exile in New Caledonia*

After her trial, imprisonment and deportation, the islands of New Caledonia became Louise Michel's home for more than six years.

In exile, Louise Michel took up teaching both French settlers and the indigenous Kanak population. She had an Enlightenment faith in reason, science and art as ennobling the condition of humanity. Throughout her life, she took a great amateur interest in scientific experiment, botany, biology and nutrition. With plenty of spare time during her exile, she conducted a range of botanical studies and scientific experiments taking extensive records of the new Pacific flora and fauna, and experimenting with the vaccination of papaya trees against jaundice.

During the 1878 Kanak revolt, most of the Communards exiled in New Caledonia rallied to the French state, but Louise Michel took up defense of the Kanak cause. Her Memoirs *highlight her antiracist sentiments and her contempt for notions of European superiority.*

Louise Michel

The Kanaks were seeking the same liberty we had sought in the Commune...

The hope for liberty and bread was in the hearts of the Kanaks. They rebelled in 1878, seeking liberty and dignity. Not all of my comrades approved of their rebellion as strongly as I did. One day Bauer and I were talking about the revolt of the Kanaks, a burning question on the Ducos peninsula. We started speaking so loudly that a guard ran over from the post office thinking that a riot had broken out. He withdrew, very disconcerted, when he saw there were only two of us.

That argument was about not only the Kanaks, but also about a Kanak play. Bauer accused me of wanting to put on a Kanak play, and I didn't deny it. We deportees had a theater on the hill above Numbo. It had its directors, its actors, its stagehands, its sets, and its board of directors. This theater was a masterpiece, given the conditions under which we were living. Every Sunday we used to go to the theater. We put on everything there: dramas, vaudeville, operettas. We even sang fragments of an opera, *Robert the Devil,* although we didn't have all the score.

True, the leading women usually had deep, booming voices, and their hands kept searching in their skirt pockets as if they were looking for a cigar. Even my court-martial dress, which was very long, left their feet uncovered to the ankles, for some of our leading ladies were tall. They lengthened their skirts finally, and then nothing was lacking in their costumes. Wolowski trained the chorus.

They were talking about an orchestra when I left the peninsula for Noumea. I had my own ideas for an orchestra: I wanted to shake palm branches, strike bamboo, create a horn from shells, and use the tones produced by a leaf pressed against the lips. In short, I wanted a Kanak orchestra, complete with quarter tones. Thanks to knowledge I had gotten from Daoumi and the Kanak who brought supplies, I believed I knew enough to try. But my plan was blocked by the Committee of Light Classical Theater. Indeed, they accused me of being a savage.

To some comrades I seemed to be more Kanak than the Kanaks. They argued a bit, so to make the situation a little more interesting, I spoke of putting on a Kanak play whose text was wearing out my pocket. I even talked about performing the play dressed in black tights and I added a few more details designed to exasperate those people: the incident took its normal course, rousing my adversaries and amusing me deep within.

The revolt of the tribes was deadly serious, but it is better if I say little about it. The Kanaks were seeking the same liberty we had sought in the Commune. Let me say only that my red scarf, the red scarf of the Commune that I had hidden from every search, was divided in two pieces one night. Two Kanaks, before going to join the insurgents against the whites, had come to say goodbye to me. They slipped into the ocean. The sea was bad, and they may never have arrived across the bay, or perhaps they were killed in the fighting. I never saw either of them again, and I don't know which of the two deaths took them, but they were brave with the bravery that black and white both have...

The Kanak Insurrection of 1878 failed. The strength and longing of human hearts was shown once again, but the whites shot down the rebels as we were mowed down in front of Bastion 37 and on the plains of Satory. When they sent Atai's head to Paris, I wondered who the real headhunters were. As Henri Rochefort had once written to me: "the Versailles Government could give the natives lessons in cannibalism"...

Early in 1879, the authorities allowed me to leave the Ducos peninsula and move to Noumea. Those who had a profession and could be self-supporting were given a measure of freedom; so I went to Noumea to teach. There I taught not only the children of the white colonists, but also the Kanaks, and among those I taught was Daoumi's brother.

It was fitting that I should teach him, because Daoumi was the first Kanak I had met in New Caledonia. After that first meeting with Daoumi, I saw him again many times. To practise European life he got a job at the canteen on the Ducos peninsula, and when I talked to him I got him to tell me the legends of the Kanakas, and he gave me vocabulary lists. For my part, I tried to tell him the things I believed it was most important for him to know. There were many legends that I learned from Daoumi and his brother.

Daoumi's brother and I also spoke of the short future that loomed before his race, when untutored and unarmed men faced our greed and our innumerable means of destruction. Seeing the lofty, resolute mind and the courageous and kind heart of Daoumi's brother, I wondered which of us was the superior being: the one who assimilates foreign knowledge through a thousand difficulties for the sake of his race, or the well-armed white who annihilates those who are less well armed. Other races giving way before our arms is no proof of our superiority. If tigers and elephants and lions suddenly covered Europe and attacked us, they would triumph in a storm of destruction and would seem superior to us.

From: Louise Michel, *Mémoires*
(Trans. —*Ed.*)

Louise Michel
Art for all! Science for all! Bread for all!

New wonders will come from science, and change must come. Time raises up volcanoes under old continents, and time allows new feelings to grow. Soon there will be neither cruelty nor exploitation, and science will provide all humanity with enough food, with nourishing food. I dream of the time when science will give everyone enough to eat. Instead of the putrefied flesh which we are accustomed to eating, perhaps science will give us chemical mixtures containing more iron and nutrients than the blood and meat we now absorb...

With the abundance of nourishing food in that future world, there must be art, too. In that coming era, the arts will be for everyone. The power of harmonious colors, the grandeur of sculpted marble — they will belong to the entire human race. Genius will be developed, not snuffed out. Ignorance has done enough harm. The privilege of knowledge is worse than the privilege of wealth.

The arts are a part of human rights, and everybody needs them. Neither music, nor marble, nor color, can by itself proclaim the Marseillaise of the new world. Who will sing out the Marseillaise of art? Who will tell of the thirst for knowledge, of the ecstasy of musical harmonies, of marble made flesh, of canvas palpitating like life? Art, like science and liberty, must be no less available than food.

Everyone must take up a torch to let the coming era walk in light. Art for all! Science for all! Bread for all!

From: Louise Michel, *Mémoires*
(Trans. —*Ed.*)

Louise Michel
Letter protesting removal from Numbo camp

Exiled to New Caledonia, the leaders of the Commune were initially detained on the Ducos peninsula at Numbo. Together with other women of the Commune, Michel refused to be separated from her male comrades.

Numbo, May 20, 1875

Deportee Louise Michel, No.1, protests against the ruling which assigns all female deportees to housing far away from the Numbo camp, as if their presence was causing a scandal. Given that the same law applies to both men and women who were deported, there is no need to add this undeserved insult.

For my part, I will not go to this new home unless the reasons for which we are being sent are made public in a poster, together with details of the manner in which we'll be treated there.

Deportee Louise Michel declares that, if the reasons for this change are an insult, she will protest right till the end, whatever happens to her.

Louise Michel, No.1

Xavière Gauthier (ed), *Louise Michel, je vous écris de ma nuit.* (Trans. —*Ed.*)

chapter eight: *Authority Vested in One Person is a Crime*

In the aftermath of the Paris Commune, tens of thousands of Communards were massacred by the troops of Versailles. Surviving leaders of the Commune, including Louise Michel, were brought before military tribunals. Michel received a sentence of lifetime deportation and was sent to the French colony of New Caledonia in the South Pacific in August 1873. After a general amnesty in 1880, Michel was pardoned.

Years of exile in New Caledonia had not dimmed her contempt of authority and she returned to France to resume her agitation. She continued to scorn arbitrary authority: in 1882, Michel was brought before a Paris court for insulting police, and in 1883 she was arrested for leading a demonstration across Paris, carrying a black flag, during which bread was taken from three bakeries.

Louise Michel

Statement to the military tribunal after the Paris Commune, 1871

I do not wish to defend myself, I do not wish to be defended. I belong completely to the social revolution and I declare that I accept complete responsibility for all my actions. I accept it completely and without reservations.

You accuse me of having taken part in the murder of the generals? To that I would reply — yes, if I had been in Montmartre when they wished to have the people fired on. I would not have hesitated to fire myself on those who gave such orders. But I do not understand why they were shot when they were prisoners, and I look on this action as arrant cowardice.

As for the burning of Paris, yes, I took part in it. I wished to oppose the invaders from Versailles with a barrier of flames. I had no accomplices in this action. I acted on my own initiative.

I am told that I am an accomplice of the Commune. Certainly, yes, since the Commune wanted more than anything else the social revolution, and since the social revolution is the dearest of my desires. More than that, I have the honor of being one of the instigators of the Commune, which by the way had nothing — nothing, as is well known — to do with murder and arson. I who was present at all the sittings at the Town Hall, I declare that there was never any question of murder or arson.

Do you want to know who are really guilty? It is the politicians. And perhaps, later, light will be brought onto all these events which today it is found quite natural to blame on all supporters of the social revolution…

But why should I defend myself? I have already declared that I refuse to do so. You are men who are going to judge me. You sit before me unmasked. You are men and I am only a woman, and yet I look you in the eye. I know quite well that everything I could say will not make the least difference to your sentence. So a single last word before I sit down. We never wanted anything but the triumph of the great principles of the revolution. I swear it on our martyrs who fell at Satory, by our martyrs whom I acclaim loudly, and who will one day have their revenge.

Once more I belong to you. Do with me as you please. Take my life if you wish. I am not the woman to argue with you for a moment...

What I claim from you, you who call yourselves a Council of War, who sit as my judges, who do not disguise yourselves as a Commission of Pardons, you who are military men and deliver your judgment in the sight of all, is Satory where our brothers have already fallen.

I must be cut off from society. You have been told to do so. Well, the Commissioner of the Republic is right. Since it seems that any heart which beats for freedom has the right only to a small lump of lead, I demand my share. If you let me live, I shall never stop crying for vengeance, and I shall avenge my brothers by denouncing the murderers in the Commission for Pardons.

President of the Court: I cannot allow you to continue speaking if you continue in this tone.

Louise Michel: I have finished... If you are not cowards, kill me.

Sixth Court Martial Board (Versailles)
Report of Louise Michel's trial for insulting police, 1882

Louise Michel was the first accused called. The valiant citizen was entirely self-possessed, and in her own voice she answered the judge's questions in a very precise manner.

"You are charged with insulting policemen," said M. Puget, the judge.

"On the contrary, it is we who should bring charges concerning brutality and insults," Louise Michel said, "because we were very peaceful. What happened, and doubtless the reason I am here, is this: I went to the headquarters of the police commissioner and when I got there, I looked out a window and saw several policemen beating a man. I did not want to say anything to those policemen because they were very overexcited, so I went up to the next floor and found two other policemen who were calmer. I said to them, 'Go down quickly. Someone is being murdered'."

The judge said: "That story does not agree with the depositions of witnesses we're about to hear."

Louise Michel answered: "What I've said is the truth. When accusations against me have been true, I've admitted things far more serious than this."

The first witness called was a police constable named Conar. He said that when he got to the police commissioner's he found two women, one of whom was Louise Michel. He testified that she said to him: "You are killers and loafers."

"That's a lie," said Louise Michel. The police constable persisted in claiming his account was true. Louise Michel repeated that she was telling the truth and could say nothing more.

Regardless of the police constable's story being a lie, the court sentenced Louise Michel to two weeks in prison for violating Article 224 of the Penal Code.

From: Report published in the newspaper
L'Intransigent. January 7, 1882.

Louise Michel
Telegram to organizers of the Les Invalides protest

In March 1883, police began searching for Louise Michel after she led a rally of unemployed people at Les Invalides in Paris, during which some bakeries were looted. She was invited to speak at a number of public meetings after the rally, but kept a low profile, as indicated in the telegram sent to meeting organizers on March 10.

Dear citizens and friends,

It seems that the police are preparing to disrupt my presentation to the meetings this evening. Please excuse me for not attending, in order to avoid giving pleasure to Mr. Camescasse [the police commissioner].

When they bring me before the courts, I will go there by myself, without the need for my friends who are defending me to be arrested as well.

Louise Michel
March 10, 1883

Xavière Gauthier (ed.), *Louise Michel, je vous écris de ma nuit.* (Trans. —*Ed.*)

Louise Michel
Les Invalides Trial, 1883

Louise's contempt for the authorities is evident in her statement to the court at her 1883 trial, after which she was sentenced to six years in solitary confinement.

What is being done to us here is a political proceeding. It isn't we who are being prosecuted, but the Anarchist Party through us...

What is surprising you, what is appalling you, is that a woman is daring to defend herself. People aren't accustomed to seeing a woman who dares to think. People would rather, as Proudhon put it, see a woman as either a housewife or a courtesan.

We carried the black flag because the demonstration was to be absolutely peaceful, and the black flag is the flag of strikes and the flag of those who are hungry. Could we have carried any other flag? The red flag is nailed up in the cemeteries, and we should take it up only when we can protect it. Well, we couldn't do that. I have told you before and now I repeat: it was an essentially peaceful demonstration.

I went to the demonstration. I had to go. Why was I arrested?... I've gone throughout Europe saying that I recognize no borders, saying that all humanity has the right to the heritage of humanity. That inheritance will not belong to us, because we are accustomed to living in slavery. It will belong to those persons in the future who will have liberty and who will know how to enjoy it.

When we are told that we are the enemies of the republic, we have only one answer: We founded it upon 35,000 of our corpses. That is how we defended the republic...

Isn't it simply a law of might makes right which is dominating us? We want to replace it with the idea that right makes right. That is the extent of our crime.

Above the courts, beyond the 20 years in prison you can sentence us to — beyond even a life sentence — I see the dawn of liberty and equality breaking.

Knowing what is going on around you, you too are tired of it, disgusted by it. How can you remain calm when you see the proletariat constantly suffering from hunger while others are gorging themselves?

We knew that the demonstration at Les Invalides would come to nothing, and yet it was necessary to go there. At this time in history we are very badly off. We do not call the regime that rules us a republic. A republic is a form of government which makes progress, where there is justice, where there is bread for all. How does the republic you have made differ from the empire? What is this talk about liberty in the courts when five years of prison waits at the end?

I do not want the cry of the workers to be lost. You will do with me what you wish, but it's a question of more than me alone. It's a matter that concerns a large part of France, a large part of the world, for people are becoming more and more anarchistic... There is no doubt that you will see still more revolutions, and for that we will march confidently toward the future.

When one person alone no longer has authority, there will be light, truth and justice. Authority vested in one person is a crime. What we want is authority vested in everyone...

People recognize homelands only to make them a foyer for war. People recognize borders only to make them an object of intrigue. We conceive homelands and family in a much broader sense. These are our crimes.

We live in an age of anxiety. Everybody is trying to find his own way, but we say anyhow that whatever happens, if liberty is realized and quality achieved, we shall be happy.

Superior court of the Seine District, June 21, 1883.

Louise Michel
Letter to the Commissioner of Police

Sir,

I have constantly protested against the infamy of being granted a pardon.

I do not know why you are inflicting this insult on me, and I declare again that I will not leave prison unless all the others are released.

Please receive my respect,

L. Michel
Saint-Lazare, January 14, 1886.

Xavière Gauthier (ed), *Louise Michel, je vous écris de ma nuit.* (Trans. —*Ed.*)

chapter nine: *Emma and Louise*

Emma Goldman — feminist, activist, organizer — was profoundly influenced by the example of Louise Michel. Born in Russia, Goldman migrated to the United States at age 16, where she lectured, wrote and protested on issues of militarism, free speech, women's rights and civil liberties.

"Red Emma" spent much of her life traveling between Europe and the United States, promoting her philosophy of anarchism. During these travels in 1895, she first met Louise Michel, whom she later described as "the priestess of pity and vengeance." In 1899, both women spoke together in London in support of the Haymarket martyrs — anarchists condemned for the death of Chicago policemen in the May Day bombing of 1886.

In her autobiography, Living my Life, *Emma Goldman spells out the impact that Louise Michel had on her life. In later polemics with other writers, she also addressed the issue of public women and homosexuality, in response to a German article about Louise and lesbianism.*

Emma Goldman
There was spirit and youth in her eyes

One of my aims in visiting England was to meet the outstanding personalities in the anarchist movement... Louise Michel I met almost immediately upon my arrival. The French comrades I stayed with had arranged a reception for my first Sunday in London. Ever since I had read about the Paris Commune, its glorious beginning and its terrible end, Louise Michel had stood out sublime in her love for humanity, grand in her zeal and courage. She was angular, gaunt, aged before her years (she was only 62) but there was spirit and youth in her eyes, and a smile so tender that it immediately won my heart.

This, then, was the woman who had survived the savagery of the respectable Paris mob. Its fury had drowned the Commune in the blood of the workers and had strewn the streets of Paris with thousands of dead and wounded. Not being appeased, it had also reached out for Louise. Again and again she had courted death; on the barricades of Père Lachaise, the last stand of the Communards, Louise had chosen the most dangerous position for herself. In court she had demanded the same penalty as was meted out to her comrades, scorning clemency on the grounds of sex. She would die for the cause.

Whether out of fear or awe of this heroic figure, the murderous Paris bourgeoisie had not dared to kill her. They preferred to doom her to a slow death in New Caledonia. But they had reckoned without the fortitude of Louise Michel, her devotion and capacity for consecration to her fellow sufferers. In New Caledonia she became the hope and inspiration of the exiles. In sickness she nursed their bodies; in depression she cheered their spirits. The amnesty for the

Communards brought Louise back with the others to France. She found herself the acclaimed idol of the French masses. They adored her as their Mère Louise, *bien aimée.* Shortly after her return from exile Louise headed a demonstration of unemployed to the Esplanade des Invalides. Thousands were out of work for a long time and hungry. Louise led the procession into the bakery shops, for which she was arrested and condemned to five years' imprisonment. In court she defended the right of the hungry man to bread, even if he has to "steal" it. Not the sentence, but the loss of her dear mother proved the greatest blow to Louise at her trial. She loved her with an absorbing affection and now she declared that she had nothing else to live for except the revolution. In 1886 Louise was pardoned, but she refused to accept any favors from the state. She had to be taken forcibly from prison in order to be set at liberty.

During a large meeting in Le Havre someone fired two shots at Louise while she was on the platform talking. One went through her hat; the other struck her behind the ear. The operation, although very painful, called forth no complaint from Louise. Instead she lamented her poor animals left alone in her rooms and the inconvenience the delay would cause her woman friend who was waiting for her in the next town. The man who nearly killed her had been influenced by a priest to commit the act, but Louise tried her utmost to have him released. She induced a famous lawyer to defend her assailant and she herself appeared in court to plead with the judge in his behalf. Her sympathies were particularly stirred by the man's young daughter, whom she could not bear to have become fatherless by the man's being sent to prison. Louise's stand did not fail to influence even her fanatical assailant.

Later Louise was to participate in a great strike in Vienna, but she was arrested at the Gare du Lyon as she was about to board the train. The cabinet member responsible for the massacre of the workingmen in Fourmies saw in Louise a formidable force that he had repeatedly tried to crush. Now he demanded her removal from jail to an insane asylum on the ground that she was deranged and dangerous. It was this fiendish plan to dispose of Louise that induced her comrades to persuade her to move to England.

The vulgar French papers continued to paint her as a wild beast, as "La Vierge Rouge" [The Red Virgin] without any feminine qualities or charm. The more decent wrote of her with bated breath. They feared her, but they also looked up to her as something far above their empty souls and hearts. As I sat near her at our first meeting, I wondered how anyone could fail to find charm in her. It was true that she cared little about her appearance. Indeed, I had never seen a woman so utterly oblivious of anything that concerned herself. Her dress was shabby, her bonnet ancient. Everything she wore was ill-fitting. But her whole being was illumined by an inner light. One quickly succumbed to the spell of her radiant personality, so compelling in its strength, so moving in its childlike simplicity. The afternoon with Louise was an experience unlike anything that had happened till then in my life. Her hand in mine, its tender pressure on my head, her words of endearment and close comradeship, made my soul expand, reach out toward the spheres of beauty where she dwelt.

From: Emma Goldman, *Living my Life*
(New York: AMS Press, 1970), 166.

Emma Goldman

Louise Michel was a complete woman

Dear Dr. Hirschfeld:

I have been acquainted with your great works on sexual psychology for a number of years now. I have always deeply admired your courageous intervention on behalf of the rights of people who are by their natural disposition unable to express their sexual feelings in what is customarily called the "normal" way. Now that I have had the pleasure of making your personal acquaintance and observing your efforts at first had, I feel more strongly than ever the impress of your personality and spirit which has guided you in your difficult undertaking.

Your willingness to place your periodical at my disposal, giving me the opportunity to present a critical evaluation of the essay by Herr von Levetzow on the alleged homosexuality of Louise Michel, is proof — if such proof were ever required — that you are a man with a deep sense of justice and interested only in the truth...

Above all, I feel obliged to preface my response to the statements of the above-mentioned author with a few brief comments. In challenging what I regard as erroneous presuppositions on the part of Herr von Levetzow, I am in no way motivated by any prejudice against homosexuality itself or any antipathy toward homosexuals in general. Had Louise Michel ever manifested any type of sexual feelings in all those relationships with people whom she loved and who were devoted to her, I would certainly be the last to seek to cleanse her of this "stigma."

It is a tragedy, I feel, that people of a different sexual type are caught in a world which shows so little understanding for homosexuals, is so crassly indifferent to the various gradations and variations of gender and their great significance in life. Far be it for me to seek to evaluate these people as inferior, less moral, or incapable of higher feelings and actions. I am the last person to whom it would occur to "protect" Louise Michel, my great teacher and comrade, from the charge of homosexuality. Louise Michel's service to humanity and her great work of social liberation are such that they can be neither enlarged nor reduced, whatever her sexual habits were.

Years ago, before I knew anything about sexual psychology and when my sole acquaintance with homosexuals was limited to a few women I had met in prison (where I was held because of my political convictions), I spoke up in no uncertain terms on behalf of Oscar Wilde. As an anarchist, my place has always been on the side of the persecuted. The entire persecution and sentencing of Wilde struck me as an act of cruel injustice and repulsive hypocrisy on the part of the society which condemned this man. And this alone was the reason which prompted me to stand up for him...

From all of this, your readers may recognize that any prejudice or antipathy toward homosexuals is totally foreign to me. On the contrary! Among my male and female friends, there are a few who are of either a completely Uranian or a bisexual disposition. I have found these individuals far above average in terms of intelligence, ability, sensitivity and personal charm. I empathize deeply with them, for I know that their sufferings are of a larger and more complex sort than those of ordinary people.

But there exists among very many homosexuals a predominant intellectual outlook which I must seriously challenge. I am speaking of the practise of claiming every possible prominent personality as one of their own, attributing their own feelings and character traits to these people.

If one were to believe the assurances and claims of many homosexuals, one would be forced to the conclusion that no truly great person is or ever was to be found outside the circle of persons of a different sexual type. Social ostracism and persecution inevitably spawn sectarianism; but this outlook, narrow in its perspective, often renders people unjust in their praise of others. Without wishing to offend Herr von Levetzow in any way, I must say that he seems to be strongly influenced by the sectarian spirit of many homosexuals, perhaps unconsciously so.

Beyond that, he has an antiquated conception of the essence of womanhood. He sees in woman a being meant by nature solely to delight man with her attractiveness, bear his children, and otherwise figure as a domestic and general household slave. Any woman who fails to meet these shopworn requirements of womanhood is promptly taken as a Uranian by this writer. In light of the accomplishments of women to date in every sector of human intellectual life and in efforts for social change, this traditional male conception of womanhood scarcely deserves regard any longer.

I nonetheless feel compelled to pursue the outmoded views of this writer concerning Louise Michel to some extent, if only to show the reader what nonsensical conclusions can be reached if one proceeds from nonsensical presuppositions…

Modern woman is no longer satisfied to be the beloved of a man; she looks for understanding, comradeship; she wants to be treated as a human being and not simply as an object for sexual gratification. And since man in many cases cannot offer her this, she turns to her sisters.

[My only desire is to see Michel] portrayed as she actually was: an extraordinary woman, a significant thinker and a profound soul. She represented a new type of womanhood which is nonetheless as old as the race, and she had a soul which was permeated by an all-encompassing and all-understanding love for humanity.

In short, Louise Michel was a complete woman, free of all the prejudices and traditions which for centuries held women in chains and degraded them to household slaves and objects of sexual lust.

The new woman celebrated her resurrection in the figure of Louise, the woman capable of heroic deeds but one who remains a woman in her passion and in her love.

From the 1923 article by Emma Goldman in the *Yearbook for Sexual Intermediate Types*, issued by the Scientific-Humanitarian Committee, Germany's leading homosexual rights organization (http://www.angelfire.com/ok/Flack/emma.html).

resources

Books in English

Bullitt Lowry and Elizabeth Ellington Gunter (eds), *The Red Virgin — Memoirs of Louise Michel* (Alabama: University of Alabama Press, 1981).

Gay Gullickson, *Unruly Women of Paris — Images of the Commune* (Ithaca: Cornell University Press, 1996).

Eugene Schulkind, "Socialist Women during the 1871 Paris Commune," *Past and Present,* No. 106 (1985).

Edith Thomas, *Louise Michel* (Montreal: Black Rose Books, 1980).

Edith Thomas, *The Women Incendiaries* (London: Secker and Warburg, 1967).

George Woodcock, *Anarchism* (London: Pelican, 1962). Especially Chapter 10: "Anarchism in France."

Books in French

Louise Michel, *Mémoires* (Arles: Editions Sulliver, 1998). Originally published in 1886.

Louise Michel, *La Commune — histoire et souvenirs* (Paris: Editions La Découverte, 1999). Originally published in 1898.

Louise Michel, *Aux amis d'Europe* et *Légendes et chansons de gestes canaques* (Noumea: Editions Grain de Sable, 1996). Originally published in 1885.

Louise Michel, *Souvenirs et aventures de ma vie* (Paris: Editions La Découverte/Maspero, 1983). Originally published in 1905.

Xavière Gauthier, *Louise Michel, je vous écris de ma nuit —
Correspondance Générale 1850–1904* (Paris: Les éditions de
Paris, 1999). Collected letters from 1850 until her death.

Xavière Gauthier, *La Vierge Rouge — biographie de Louise
Michel* (Paris: Les éditions de Paris, 1999)

Christine Roibeyreix, *Louise Michel quand l'aurore se levera*
(Perigueux: La Lauze, 2002).

Edith Thomas, *Les Petroleuses* (Paris: Gallimard, 1963).

Edith Thomas, *Louise Michel ou la Velleda de l'Anarchie* (Paris:
Gallimard, 1971).

On the Paris Commune

Stewart Edwards, *The Paris Commune, 1871* (London: Eyre and
Spottiswoode, 1971).

Karl Marx, *The Civil War in France* (Beijing: Foreign Language
Press, 1971).

Karl Marx and Friedrich Engels: *On the Paris Commune* (Moscow:
Progress Press, 1971).

Jacques Rougerie, *Paris Insurgé — la Commune de 1871* (Paris:
Découvertes Gallimard, 1995).

Eugene Schulkind (ed), *The Paris Commune of 1871 — The View
From the Left* (London: Jonathon Cape, 1972).

Websites and Film

The Siege and Commune of Paris, 1870–71:
http://www.library.northwestern.edu/spec/siege/
This site contains links to over 1,200 digitized photographs and
images recorded during the Siege and Commune of Paris c.1871.
The Library's Siege & Commune Collection contains 1,500
caricatures, 68 newspapers in hard copy and film, hundreds of

books and pamphlets and about 1,000 posters.

Paris Commune website:
http://www.arts.unsw.edu.au/pariscommune/index.html
Includes extracts from Australian newspapers reporting on the
Commune.

Anarchy archives links:
http://dwardmac.pitzer.edu/anarchist_archives/pariscommune/
Pariscommunehistory.html

Karl Marx's *The Civil War in France:*
http://www.marxists.org/archive/marx/works/1871/civil-war-france/
index.htm

In French — background from Louise Michel High School:
http://www.ac-creteil.fr/Louise/louise/louise.htm

In French — good list of websites about Louise:
http://enjolras.free.fr/liens.html
http://melior.univ-montp3.fr/ra_forum/fr/individus/michel_louise/
index_f.html

British director Peter Watkins has produced an ambitious
345-minute film, *La Commune (Paris 1871)*, available on DVD and
video. For further information, see Part III of Peter Watkins film site:
http://www.peterwatkins.lt/varyk.htm

rebel lives

albert einstein
edited by Jim Green

"What I like most about Albert
Einstein is that he was a
troublemaker." —Fred Jerome,
author of *The Einstein File*

You don't have to be Einstein...
to know that he was a giant in
the world of science and
physics. Yet this book takes a
new, subversive look at *Time*
magazine's "Person of the
Century," whose passionate
opposition to war and racism
and advocacy of human rights
put him on the FBI's files as a
socialist enemy of the state.

ISBN 1-876175-63-X

sacco & vanzetti
edited by John Davis

"Sacco and Vanzetti died
because they were anarchists...
because they believed and
preached human brotherhood
and freedom. As such, they
could expect neither justice nor
humanity." —Emma Goldman

An illuminating example of
how immigrants, anarchists and
communists were the
"terrorists" of yesteryear, Nicola
Sacco and Bartolomeo Vanzetti
were convicted in a trial steeped
in racial and ideological
prejudice. Their case sparked an
unprecedented defense
campaign and became a symbol
of the international struggle for
justice, equality and liberty.

ISBN 1-876175-85-0

rebel lives

haydée santamaría
edited by Betsy Maclean

"Haydée Santamaría signifies a
world, an attitude, a sensibility as
well as a revolution."
— Mario Benedetti

Haydée first achieved notoriety as
one of two women who
participated in the armed attack
that sparked the Cuban
Revolution. Later, as director of
the world-renowned literary
institution, Casa de las Américas,
she embraced culture as a tool for
social change and provided refuge
for exiled Latin American artists
and intellectuals.

**Includes reflections by
Ariel Dorfman, Eduardo
Galeano, Alicia Alonso and
Silvio Rodríguez.**

ISBN 1-876175-59-1

helen keller
edited by John Davis

"I have entered the fight against
the economic system in which
we live. It is to be a fight to the
finish and I ask no quarter."
— Helen Keller

Poor little blind girl or
dangerous radical? This book
challenges the sanitized image
of Helen Keller, restoring her
true history as a militant
socialist. Here are her views on
women's suffrage, her defense
of the Industrial Workers of
the World, her opposition to
World War I and her support
for imprisoned socialist and
anarchist leaders, as well as her
analysis of disability and class.

ISBN 1-876175-60-5

oceanpress

e-mail info@oceanbooks.com.au
www.oceanbooks.com.au